SYBEX

OFFICIAL
strategies & secrets

D1709321

STAR TREK
STARFLEET COMMAND
III

NCC-1701-E

David Ellis

SYBEX

San Francisco • London

ASSOCIATE PUBLISHER: **Dan Brodnitz**

CONTRACTS AND LICENSING MANAGER: **Monica Baum**

ACQUISITIONS AND DEVELOPMENTAL EDITOR: **Willem Knibbe**

EDITOR: **Laura Ryan**

PRODUCTION EDITOR: **Kelly Winquist**

PROOFREADER: **Tricia Toney**

BOOK DESIGN: **Diana Van Winkle, Van Winkle Design**

BOOK PRODUCTION: **Diana Van Winkle, Van Winkle Design**

COVER DESIGN: **Victor Arre, RGraphics**

Library of Congress Control Number: 2002113633

ISBN: 0-7821-4196-X

Manufactured in the United States of America

10 9 8 7 6 5 4 3 2 1

To Kang—a great rottweiler who more than lived up to his warrior name. I miss you, my friend.

Acknowledgments

As always, there are lots of people to thank for making this book possible. Thanks to everyone at Sybex—Willem Knibbe (who always lets me know when there's a book available), Kelly Winquist, and Liz Burke. You make writing books too easy! Thanks also to Diana Van Winkle for her beautiful design and Laura Ryan for her great copy editing. And much appreciation goes to Justin Berenbaum at Activision and all the folks at Taldren for putting up with all my questions and requests—you helped me make this guide the best it could possibly be.

Thanks, also, to Activision's Dan Hagerty, Doug Mirabello, Jenny Stornetta, Kevin Wynne, Marilena Rixford, Sion Gibson, Brad Saavedra, Stacy Rivas, and Dan Siskin. I also must thank Paramount's Harry Lang and Dan Felts.

Finally, as always, thanks to my wife, Meghan, who always believes in me no matter what.

Contents

Introduction . . . . **xv**

1 TAKING THE CENTER SEAT— COMMAND BASICS 1

The View Screen **2**

   Top-Down Mode 2

   Centered Ship and Target View Modes 2

   Normal Mode 3

   Camera Lock on Target (F5) 4

Maneuverability and Speed **4**

   Alert Status 5

Bridge Systems Overview **5**

   Power Management 5

   Helm Controls 6

   Science Systems 8

   Tractor Systems 10

   Transporter Systems 10

   Shuttlecraft 10

   Scanners and Communications 11

Ship Schematic Display **11**

   System Status and Firing Arcs 11

   Damage Control 12

2 SECURITY OPS— WEAPONS OVERVIEW 13

Primary Weapons 14
   Federation Primary Weapons (Phasers) 14
   Klingon and Romulan Primary Weapons (Disruptors) 16
   Borg Primary Weapons (Cutting Beams) 18
Heavy Weapons 19
   Federation Heavy Weapons 19
   Klingon Heavy Weapons 20
   Romulan Heavy Weapons 22
   Borg Heavy Weapons 23
   Tachyon Pulse 25
   Mines 25

3 ADVANCED TACTICAL TRAINING 27

General Combat Tactics 28
   Shields—Yours and Theirs 28
   The *Top Gun* Maneuver 29
   Grouping Weapons 30
   The Alpha-Strike 30
   Don't Forget Your Other Weapons 31
   Targeting Individual Systems 31
   Fleet Tactics 32
Warp Drive in Combat 33
   Warp Jumping 33
   Strafing Runs 33
Fun with Mines 34
Shuttlecraft 35
The Cloaking Device 36
   Anticloaking Tactics 37

Tractor Beams **38**

Send in the Marines **39**

    Hit-and-Run Raids 39

    Capturing Enemy Targets 40

Dealing with the Environment **40**

4 THE UNITED FEDERATION OF PLANETS 43

Saber-Class "Frigate" **44**

Norway-Class "Destroyer" **45**

Defiant-Class "Light Cruiser" **46**

Intrepid-Class "Light Cruiser" **47**

Akira-Class "Heavy Cruiser" **48**

Excelsior-Class "Heavy Cruiser" **49**

Nebula-Class "Battlecruiser" **50**

Galaxy-Class "Dreadnought" **51**

Sovereign-Class "Battleship" **52**

5 THE KLINGON EMPIRE 53

Bird of Prey (B'rel)-Class "Frigate" **54**

K'Vort-Class "Destroyer" **55**

K'Tinga-Class "Light Cruiser". **56**

Fek'Ihr-Class "Heavy Cruiser" **57**

Vor'cha-Class "Heavy Battlecruiser" **58**

Negh'var-Class "Battleship" **59**

6 THE ROMULAN STAR EMPIRE.... 61

Talon-Class "Frigate" 62
Falcon-Class "Destroyer" 63
Shrike-Class "Light Cruiser" 64
Hawk-Class "Heavy Cruiser" 65
Raptor-Class "Heavy Battlecruiser" 66
Warbird (D'Deridex)-Class "Battleship" 67

7 THE BORG COLLECTIVE.... 69

Pyramid 70
Pyramid Prime 71
Diamond 72
Diamond Prime 73
Sphere 74
Sphere Prime 75
Cube 76

8 SPACE DOCK— STARSHIP DESIGN 79

Design Basics 80
Customizable Systems 81
   Shields 83
   Primary Weapons 84
   Heavy Weapons 86
   Hull Systems 87
   Bridge Systems 88
   Engines 89

Ships on a Budget **91**

   Ships Under 30,000 Points 92

   37,000- to 50,000-Point Ships 94

Ships of the Line **96**

   USS Enterprise (NCC-1701D) 96

   USS Enterprise (NCC-1701E) 97

   USS Voyager (NCC-74656) 98

   USS Defiant (NX-74205) 99

   I.K.V. Rotarran 100

9 COMMAND DECISIONS 101

Exploring the Galaxy **102**

   Environmental Factors 102

   Enemy Activity 102

   Non-Core Missions 104

Prestige **104**

   Promotions and Awards 104

Space Dock **105**

   Repairing Your Ship 105

   Restocking Your Ship 105

   Refitting Your Ship 106

   Replacing Your Ship 107

   Recruiting Your Crew 108

10 THE KLINGON CAMPAIGN 111

Mission 1—Brotherhood 112
Mission 2—A Vast Ye Scurvy Targs 113
Mission 3—A Base Too Far 114
Mission 4—Search and Rescue 115
Mission 5—Winds of Change 116
Mission 6—Anvil of Peace 117
Mission 7—Turning the Tables 118
Mission 8—Fish in a Barrel 119
Mission 9—Obedience 120
Mission 10—Errant Duty 121
Mission 11—And Two Come Barking 122
Mission 12—Father's Day 123
Mission 13—Friend or Foe? 124
Mission 14—Recall Your Brother 125
Mission 15—To Hunt One's Blood 126

11 THE ROMULAN CAMPAIGN 129

Mission 1—Look under Every Rock 130
Mission 2—The Sound of Victory 131
Mission 3—Profit Motive 132
Mission 4—Dark Water 133
Mission 5—Tip-Toe Among Giants 134
Mission 6—The Ultimate Duty 135
Mission 7—Quietly I Step 136
Mission 8—Sneakers 137
Mission 9—Klingon Maru 138
Mission 10—Gray Area 139
Mission 11—Herding Cats 140
Mission 12—The Barrows 140
Mission 13—Shiny New Toy 141

Mission 14—You Can't Make Me Eat *Gagh!* 142
Mission 15—In Sheep's Clothing 143
Mission 16—Trojan Horse 144
Mission 17—Salt the Ground 145

12 THE FEDERATION CAMPAIGN . . . 147

Mission 1—One Big, Happy Fleet 148
Mission 2—Rendezvous at Khitomer 149
Mission 3—Warm Reception 150
Mission 4—The Stakeout 151
Mission 5—Terran: Incognito 152
Mission 6—Counterstroke 154
Mission 7—Forced Entry 155
Mission 8—Operation Roundup 156
Mission 9—Elusive Quarry 157
Mission 10—A Lightly Scorched Empire 158
Mission 11—The Luddite Syndrome 159
Mission 12—The Point of No Return 160

13 GENERAL CAMPAIGN MISSIONS AND CONQUEST CAMPAIGNS . . . 163

Base Assault 164
Convoy Assault 165
Distress Call 166
Patrol 167
    Attacked! 167
Planetary Assault 168
Scan 169
Shipyard Assault 169
Conquest Campaigns 170

14 SKIRMISH MISSIONS 171

Base Assault 172
Battlefest 173
Free for All 175
Team Assault 176

15 DYNAVERSE 3 179

What to Expect in the Dynaverse 180
Goals and Victory Conditions 180
Dynaverse Missions 181
Fleets 182
Refits and Ship Upgrades 183
    Surviving the Ship Auction 183
    Buying Bases 184

APPENDIX: NON-PLAYER CRAFT AND INSTALLATIONS 185

Introduction

Welcome to *Starfleet Command III*. It's the late 24th century. and you have just been drafted to combat a nemesis that threatens to disrupt the fragile peace and bring chaos to the Alpha and Beta quadrants. At your disposal are a myriad of state-of-the-art starships and the finest weaponry and personnel in the galaxy. A lot of this is going to be new to you, and there's no time for years of formal academy training—but fear not! You hold in your hands a training guide that gives you the information you need to prevail against this threat and restore order.

HOW TO USE THIS BOOK

Captaining starships is not something that comes naturally, so there's a lot of information to cover. We've structured this book so you can easily find and assimilate the information you need most.

Chapter 1: Taking the Center Seat—Command Basics discusses the fundamentals of controlling your ship—skills that apply to any mission or combat situation.

Chapter 2: Security Ops—Weapons Overview provides a complete tactical analysis of every weapon in the game.

In **Chapter 3: Advanced Tactical Training,** we take an in-depth look at combat using specific combat examples and situations. You'll learn great tricks and tactics, including tractor beam uses, the nuances of mine warfare, fleet tactics, and marine combat.

Chapters 4 through 7 provide you with tactical analyses of all the ships you can control in the game. Each chapter focuses on a specific empire:

Chapter 4: The United Federation of Planets

Chapter 5: The Klingon Empire

Chapter 6: The Romulan Star Empire

Chapter 7: The Borg Collective

A new twist offered in *Starfleet Command III* is the ability to design and refit starships. **Chapter 8: Space Dock—Starship Design** gives you all the information you need to adjust your ships and systems to suit the needs of a particular campaign mission or tear up your opponents in a skirmish.

The next five chapters give you an in-depth look at campaign strategies and walk you through all the missions in the single-player campaign.

In **Chapter 9: Command Decisions,** you get a basic overview of the tasks you need to perform between campaign duty assignments, including an overview of the prestige system and tactics for recruiting and retaining the best starship crews in the fleet.

The single-player campaign is played out in three parts, each of which focuses on the activities of one of the "big three" Alpha Quadrant empires:

Chapter 10: The Klingon Campaign provides a walkthrough of the core Klingon missions.

Chapter 11: The Romulan Campaign provides a walkthrough of the core Romulan missions.

Chapter 12: The Federation Campaign provides a walkthrough of the core Federation missions.

Not all the missions you encounter in the single-player campaign are part of the core campaign progression. **Chapter 13: General Campaign Missions and Conquest Campaigns** provides you with walkthroughs of the typical non-core missions you will encounter as you play through each campaign.

Chapter 14: Skirmish Missions delves into the non-campaign, instant-action missions that are available in both single- and multiplayer modes. Complete mission overviews and suggested strategies for every skirmish mission are included.

Chapter 15: Dynaverse 3 discusses the strategies and tactics that apply to *Starfleet Command III*'s massively multiplayer Dynaverse game.

Finally, the **Appendix** lists the statistics for all of the nonplayer ships and installations you'll encounter in the game.

WHAT'S IN AND WHAT'S OUT— A VETERAN'S GUIDE

If you're a *Starfleet Command* veteran, you're in for some surprises in *Starfleet Command III*. New ships, weapons, and game mechanics add a whole slew of new tactical possibilities, and feature changes and modifications render many tried-and-true strategies and tactics obsolete.

What follows is a basic summary of the features added and removed in *SFC3* that are most likely to affect your established strategies and tactics.

What's In

The 24th century: *SFC3* features the powerful ships, weapons, and equipment from *Star Trek: The Next Generation* as opposed to hardware from the *Star Trek* movie era.

New weapon systems: Many new variants of existing *Starfleet Command* weapons, such as phasers and disruptors, are now available, in addition to an impressive arsenal of new weaponry.

Warp drive and reverse thrust: The addition of warp drive and retrograde movement opens up a whole new dimension of combat tactics.

The command crew: The statistics and experience of your command crew directly affect your ship's performance and capabilities.

Streamlined shields: Deflector shields are divided into four sections instead of six, and reinforcement is a more straightforward process.

Simplified power management: Power is now divided among only three basic system groups—movement, weapons, and shields—and is easily adjustable.

What's Out

A number of star empires: The Lyrans, Gorns, Hydrans, Mirak, Interstellar Concordium, and the Orion cartels (and their associated weaponry and vessels) are no longer available.

Plasma torpedoes: At least as you know them. Plasma torpedoes are now direct-fire weapons that do not degrade over distance and cannot be shot down.

Missiles: Missiles (drones) are no longer available.

Transporter mines: Mines can no longer be transported; they can only be dropped.

Specialized shuttlecraft: No more suicide, scatterpack, or wild-weasel shuttles. All ships carry only armed administrative shuttlecraft.

Fighters: Apart from their standard shuttlecraft, starships no longer carry fighter craft.

1

Taking the Center Seat— Command Basics

Controlling a starship can be a daunting task. Even in times of peace, a starship captain is called on to make hundreds of decisions that affect the lives and well-being of your crew and, in some extreme cases, the fate of the known galaxy. As captain, you must be prepared to take command of any situation and deal with it quickly and competently. To do so, you must know every system of your ship inside and out.

This chapter gives you a crash course in basic starship operations—visual displays, control systems, energy allocation, and sensor systems. The hard-core stuff—combat operations and tactics—we'll leave for Chapter 3. You have to understand the basics of command before you can tackle a red alert situation.

Starfleet Command veterans should take the time to peruse the basic control systems since many of them have changed significantly from previous versions of the game.

THE VIEW SCREEN

"Does anyone remember when we were explorers?"—Jean-Luc Picard

Starships are equipped with sensors and scanners that provide you with a vast array of information and tactical data, however, electronic sensing devices cannot substitute for your *own* senses. The View screen is your eye on the universe, and it has a number of display modes, each of which is designed for different battle situations.

Top-Down Mode

The top-down vantage point is ideal when you're up against cloaked opponents (see Figure 1.1). By switching to Top-Down mode and zooming out slightly while the enemy is invisible, you can see the enemy ship as soon as it starts to decloak no matter where it is in relation to your vessel.

Centered Ship and Target View Modes

Centered Ship mode centers the camera on your target and tracks it (see Figure 1.2). This mode is useful for checking enemy activities at range. In a mission in which you're charged with protecting allied ships, for example, you can cycle through your enemies and see which ones pose the most imminent threat to the ship you're protecting.

Target View mode is a cross between the Centered Ship and Normal modes. Target View mode doesn't offer the freedom of camera movement available in Centered Ship mode.

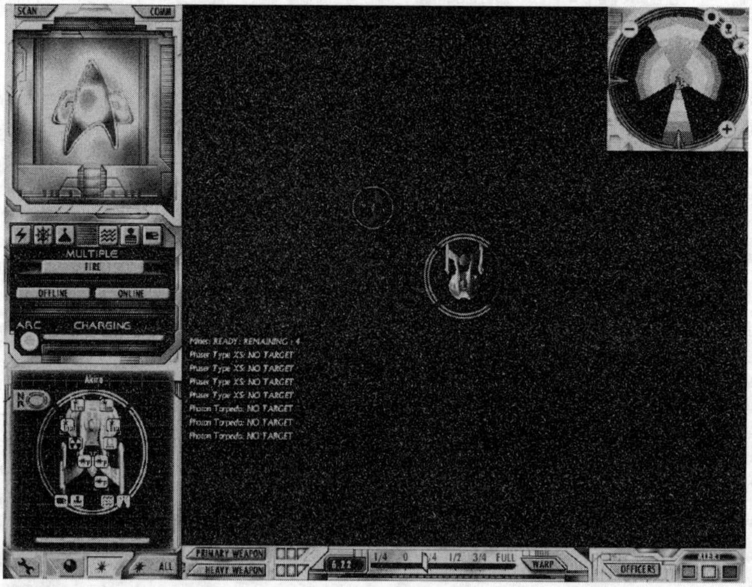

Figure 1.1 View screen in Top-Down mode

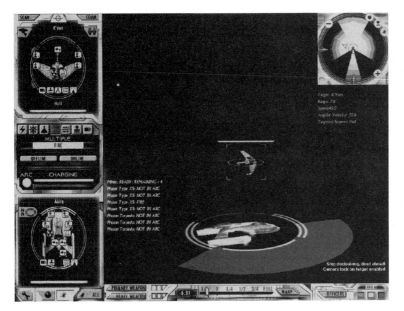

Figure 1.2 View screen in Centered Ship mode

TIP

After selecting a target in Centered Ship mode, make sure you switch to another mode (preferably Top-Down or Normal) before you engage the enemy. It is nearly impossible to issue navigation orders in Centered Ship mode.

Normal Mode

Normal mode (the default View screen mode) tends to be the most useful when you're engaged in combat (see Figure 1.3). The only time this viewpoint presents a problem is when your enemy is cloaked and manages to get behind you. Because the camera keeps your ship locked in position near the bottom of the screen, your view aft is limited, and you can't see an enemy that decloaks astern until you achieve a target lock.

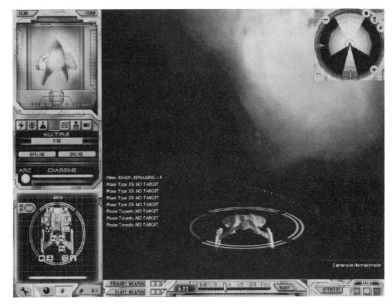

Figure 1.3 View screen in Normal mode

Camera Lock on Target (F5)

By default, the camera stays locked on your target regardless of your view mode. When you disable the camera lock, the Top-Down, Centered Ship, and Target View modes center on your ship (making the latter two modes all but useless).

The only time you should consider disabling camera lock is to survey the area from long range in Normal mode. This allows you to "look" in the direction you're heading at all times rather than keeping your eye on your target. When you're within firing range of a target, camera lock on target should *always* be active.

MANEUVERABILITY AND SPEED

Every starship has three types of engines, each of which performs a different function:

- Thrusters
- Impulse engines
- Warp Drive

Thrusters provide maneuvering power for your ship. Your ship's responsiveness is governed not only by the type of thruster it is equipped with, but also by the mass of the ship. Massive ships maneuver more sluggishly than smaller ones.

NOTE

There are a number of preprogrammed maneuvers you can use to supplement manual maneuvering in mission situations. See "Helm Controls" later in this chapter for details.

Your speed also determines how fast you can come about. When standing still or moving at high speed, it takes longer to make a turn than it does when you're moving at moderate speeds.

Impulse engines govern your ship's maximum speed and acceleration in most mission situations. As is true with thrusters, better engines produce higher speeds and better performance—but the mass of the ship is a factor when it comes to top speed, acceleration, and deceleration. Generally speaking, smaller ships perform better in all categories than their more massive counterparts. Warp drive allows your ship to travel faster than the speed of light. Normally, warp drive is used to move over great distances, but you can use it in small bursts during combat or, in extreme situations, to escape the combat area. It takes a few moments to achieve warp speed and to decelerate when you deactivate the warp drive, so plan your warp jumps accordingly.

WARNING

When you're traveling at warp speed, your shields are down and you're vulnerable to attack. If you use warp drive in combat, plan your course carefully to avoid enemy weapons arcs or you might sustain serious damage.

Alert Status

In the lower-right corner of the screen is your alert status indicator. You should *always* be at red alert—shields up, weapons active—in any mission situation.

BRIDGE SYSTEMS OVERVIEW

There is a lot more to commanding a starship than simply maneuvering and controlling your speed. In the center of the bridge systems panel on the left side of the screen is a multifunction display (MFD) that provides access to a variety of additional ship functions.

Power Management

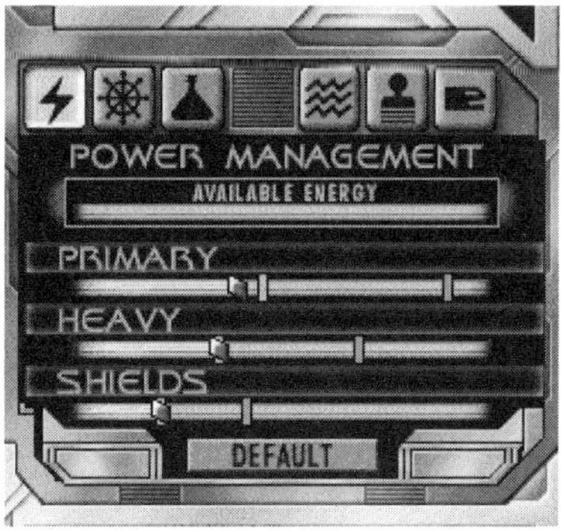

Good power management is the key to optimum ship performance in combat. The Power Management display (see Figure 1.4) shows the total amount of power available from your warp engines and provides you with an interface to distribute that power between three system categories:

Primary: Energy used to charge your primary weapons—phasers, disruptors, and so on.

Heavy: Energy used to charge your heavy weapons—photon torpedoes, plasma torpedoes, and so on.

Shields: Energy used to power and reinforce your shields.

Figure 1.4 The Power Management display

In most cases, the default energy allocation works fairly well, although in most ship designs, there is some warp energy to spare. If the Available Energy indicator shows that there is available warp power, allocate this power to one of the three systems. If at all possible, make sure the power level of each system is at least at the green mark.

Let your ship's condition be your guide when adjusting power levels in mid-battle. When weapon systems are destroyed in battle, immediately divert power from the destroyed system to the other weapon system or to the shields.

> **TIP**
>
> *If you have excess energy, allocating most of it to your shields is usually your best bet. Extra power to the shields provides an immediate increase in shield strength and a noticeable increase in regeneration rate, whereas small increases in weapon power beyond the green indicator usually have little noticeable effect in weapon efficiency.*

Helm Controls

The helm controls provide you with a number of automatic and advanced maneuvering options that supplement manual helm control (see Figure 1.5).

Automatic Maneuvering Controls

The automatic maneuvering controls are either shortcuts for performing common maneuvering functions or preprogrammed automated maneuvers that are difficult to achieve through manual control. (See the game manual for a description of each maneuver.)

Figure 1.5 The Helm Controls display

 Orbit Target: This maneuver is good for maintaining distance from a large, stationary target (such as a base or planet), but it doesn't work well when the target is moving. In combat, Orbit Target isn't a good maneuver, since it tends to expose one shield to the target at all times.

 Follow Target: This maneuver is ideal for escort missions where you must follow a target vessel to a designated destination, and works best in conjunction with the Match Target Speed command.

TIP

Never attempt a Follow Target maneuver when your target is more maneuverable than you are. If you do, the target ends up running circles around you while your ship spins hopelessly in place trying to match the target's course.

 Match Target Speed: When you select this command, the computer dynamically compensates for target speed as best it can. If the target is moving faster than your top speed, however, the computer simply sets your speed to full.

 Maximum Speed: This command is great for pursuing escaping ships or zooming to the scene of a battle when a warp jump would cause you to overshoot your destination.

 Erratic Maneuver: The purpose of this maneuver is to keep a pursuing enemy from concentrating firepower on a single shield (usually when you're running away). In most cases, manual maneuvering accomplishes this task more efficiently.

 Steady As She Goes: This control cancels any and all active automatic maneuvering and maintains your current course and speed.

 All Stop: The opposite of the Maximum Speed command, All Stop sets your velocity to zero so that you coast to a stop.

Emergency Stop: This command immediately stops you dead in space. After an Emergency Stop, you cannot engage impulse or warp engines for a short time. You can use this maneuver to get a pursuing enemy off your tail and into your forward weapons arc in an instant. Just remember you're a sitting duck until your drive systems recover, so make your shot count.

 Warp: Another way to go to warp.

High Energy Turns

High Energy Turns (HETs) require a great deal of energy and place tremendous stress on your ship's systems. When the maneuver succeeds, it gives you several seconds of lightning-fast maneuvering capability. When it fails, your engines and weapons shut down for a short time, rendering your starship temporarily helpless.

SFC veterans should note that HETs work differently in *SFC3*. Previously, there were several different forms of HET that automatically changed your heading, including one option that automatically turned your ship 180 degrees around.

HETs in *SFC3* are manually controlled. When the maneuver is initiated, you have several seconds of enhanced maneuvering capability that allow you to come about to any heading almost instantly. The maneuvering time remaining is displayed on the HET panel (see Figure 1.6). As soon as the HET energy is depleted, maneuvering returns to normal. Plan your maneuvers ahead of time to maximize the effectiveness of the HET.

The display below the HET button shows your chance for successfully completing the maneuver. Unless you're facing an extreme emergency, you shouldn't attempt an HET when the chance for success is less than 100 percent. The consequences far outweigh the benefits.

It is important to note that you're not always able to perform HETs. Your ability to do so and your chance for success depend on the skills of your helm officer (see Chapter 9 for details).

WARNING

There is no way to abort an HET once it begins, so be sure you check your chance for success before you commit to the maneuver. And be careful where you're clicking on the Helm Controls panel lest you launch into an HET by accident. The results can be disastrous.

Figure 1.6 A High Energy Turn in progress

Science Systems

Access the Science Systems control panel to launch probes, scan for cloaked ships, use your passive sensor systems, and activate your cloaking device (if you have one). The Science Systems panel also provides access to your ship's self-destruct system (see Figure 1.7).

Passive Sensors

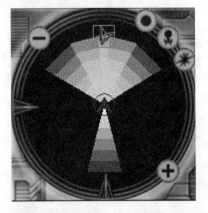

Figure 1.7 The Science Systems display

Passive sensors are operational by default. You can shut them down if you prefer, but since they draw no power and don't penalize you in any way, there's no need to disable this valuable information source.

Your ship is always centered on the Passive Sensor display. The screen has several display modes that you can toggle on and off by clicking the appropriate icons.

 Weapon range/firing arcs. These are the triangular fields projecting from your ship. The color of the arcs denotes weapon status. Red indicates that the weapons in a given arc aren't ready to fire. Yellow indicates that the weapons are ready but there is no target in the weapon's range. Green means that the weapons are ready to fire and a target is within the weapon's range.

 Targets. Other vessels and bases are indicated by colored triangles on the Passive Sensor display. (See the game manual for details.)

Planets. Planets and asteroids in the sector are displayed in miniature.

At minimum zoom, you can see the red lines that define the edges of your sector. Knowing where the nearest border is at all times lets you know which way to run if you need to escape, and keeps you from leaving the sector prematurely by making a high-speed run in the wrong direction.

Probes

Probes are used to gather data from a distance, alleviating the need for you to enter sensor range to retrieve information. Probes are only useful at extreme range. At ranges of less than 100, you gather data on most targets automatically. Probes can also be used to detect cloaked ships.

Anticloak Scan

In *SFC3,* cloaking devices are far more formidable than they were in the previous *SFC* games. Cloaking is now absolute: you can't see a cloaked ship, and you can't lock weapons on it.

That's where the anticloak scan comes in. Ships equipped with a type-IV or higher computer can send out at regular intervals a sonar-like pulse that has a chance of detecting the position of a cloaked ship, allowing you to lock weapons on it. Although the scan doesn't always detect your enemy, any chance to detect and fire on a cloaked vessel is worth the effort.

There is no penalty of any type for using the anticloak scan (including energy drain), so if your ship is so equipped, you should ping away whenever you're fighting cloaked opponents.

Self-Destruct

Self-destruct is a pretty straightforward concept. It's a last-ditch effort by which, when you're seconds from death, you attempt to inflict one last bit of pain on your worthy opponent (see Figure 1.8).

Self-destruct is considerably more powerful in *SFC3* than in the previous *SFC* games. If you time your demise so that you're at point-blank range (range 0 to 1), you can take down the shields of a heavy ship or inflict considerable internal damage on a smaller vessel.

You should only consider self-destructing in team-based multiplayer games and in Battlefest games when you have additional ships remaining. In single-player, you gain only hollow satisfaction from the act.

Self-destruct sequence in progress:2
Self-destruct sequence in progress:1
Player's Enterprise E has been destroyed!
Mission incomplete.
Press 'T' to spectate.

Figure 1.8 It is a good day to die.

Cloaking Device

In *SFC3*, all Klingon and Romulan vessels are equipped with cloaking devices. As mentioned earlier, the cloaking device in this game is considerably more potent than in previous *SFC* games. For offensive and defensive tactics related to the cloaking device, see Chapter 3.

Tractor Systems

The Tractor Systems panel contains all of the controls for your tractor beam (see Figure 1.9). Tractor beams are strictly offensive and support systems in *SFC3:* since there are no missiles in the game, there are no defensive tractors.

For tractor beam combat tactics, see Chapter 3.

Figure 1.9 The Tractor Systems panel

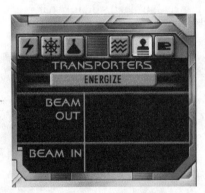

Figure 1.10 The Transporter Systems panel

Transporter Systems

The Transporter Systems panel controls your ship's transporters, primarily in noncombat missions that require you to beam items or passengers to and from designated destinations (see Figure 1.10).

When you use the transporters, the shield facing the transporter origin/destination automatically drops for several seconds while the transport takes place. Transporter operations in combat situations require precision timing and good judgment to prevent massive damage to the ship.

Transporters are also used to beam marines to enemy vessels for combat missions. For marine combat tactics, see Chapter 3.

Shuttlecraft

Shuttlecraft operations are greatly simplified in *SFC3*. Specialized shuttles and fighters are no longer available. There is only one shuttlecraft type: an advanced version of the administrative shuttle from the previous *SFC* games. Shuttlecraft launch and combat orders are issued from the Shuttlecraft control panel (see Figure 1.11).

For shuttlecraft combat tactics, see Chapter 3.

Figure 1.11 The Shuttlecraft control panel

Scanners and Communications

Scanners and communications round out the bridge controls. Unlike most bridge systems, these two functions are not accessed from the MFD, but from control buttons located above the Target Information display.

Scanners are used to obtain information on objects, planets, and vessels that probes cannot gather. Scanners draw a nominal amount of energy from your warp drive, so be sure to deactivate your scanners when you're finished scanning.

Communications are handled through a simple menu system. You can contact and communicate with friendly ships, issue fleet commands, access mission objectives, and read the captain's log. When other ships attempt to contact you, the comm system activates automatically.

For information fleet tactics, see Chapter 3.

SHIP SCHEMATIC DISPLAY

Data on your ship's vital systems is shown in the ship schematic located below the MFD (see Figure 1.12). From here you can monitor the status of your systems and perform a number of important ship functions.

System Status and Firing Arcs

Two of the three display modes on the ship schematic are primarily weapons related. Figure 1.12 shows the ship schematic in System Status mode.

Figure 1.12 The Ship Schematic display (System Status mode)

Weapon icons show whether or not your weapons are charged. If the icon is bright green, the weapon is charged and ready to fire. If the icon is dull green, the weapon has fired and is cycling (recharging).

This mode also allows you to survey your ship's weapon and system operational status. The systems are color-coded to denote their current condition:

Green indicates that a system is fully operational.

Yellow indicates that a system is damaged but still partially operational.

Red indicates that a system is badly damaged and only intermittently operational.

Gray indicates that the system is completely offline.

You can perform several weapon and shield-related operations in System Status mode:

Activate/deactivate individual weapons. To activate a single weapon, click it. To activate multiple weapons, hold down the Ctrl key and click each weapon you want to select. (For more information on weapon selection and grouping, see Chapter 3.)

Reinforce shields. Click a shield to reinforce it. A white bar indicates which shield is currently reinforced.

Deactivate shield reinforcement. Click the NR button to deactivate shield reinforcement.

Also displayed in System Status mode is your hull integrity indicator, a bar at the bottom of the display that shows the current condition of your hull. As your hull is damaged, the bar decreases to the left.

Firing Arc mode allows you to perform all of the same functions that you can perform in System Status mode, but your weapon icons are overlaid with graphics showing the firing arcs of each weapon (see Figure 1.13).

Although it is a good idea to familiarize yourself with your firing arcs, you should keep the ship schematic in System Status mode most of the time. The firing arc overlays hide the weapon icons so that you can't see their current charge and operational status.

Figure 1.13 The Ship Schematic display (Firing Arc mode)

Damage Control

In Damage Control mode, the ship system schematic allows you to repair damaged systems. Unlike the System Status mode, Damage Control mode shows only the icons of systems that require repair (see Figure 1.14).

You have only a limited number of spare parts in your stores, so if damage is widespread, you need to prioritize your repairs based on the importance of the system and the severity of the damage. Use the damage queue when multiple systems need repair, placing the top-priority systems earliest in the queue. The speed of the repair is determined in part by your chief engineer's skill (see Chapter 9 for details).

Figure 1.14 The Ship System schematic (Damage Control mode)

TIP

When you have to pick between which weapon systems to repair, always choose primary weapons over heavy. Primary weapons charge more quickly, so you're bound to get in more shots with them than with most heavy weapons. If you have to choose between primary weapons, always give priority to those with the best firing arcs.

Security Ops— Weapons Overview

Before you take your ship into battle, learn everything you can about weapons. Knowing the advantages and limitations of your armament and those of your enemy allows you to formulate strategies that take advantage of your strengths and your enemy's weaknesses.

This chapter provides you with the latest tactical data on the weapons currently deployed by every major empire in the Alpha, Beta, and Delta quadrants. Read this chapter and you should be ready to take your ship into hostile territory with confidence.

PRIMARY WEAPONS

> *"You do remember how to fire phasers?"—William Riker*

Primary weapons are your first line of defense. Regardless of which empire you play, these are the weapons that you use most often in combat—usually because they are the fastest and the most reliable.

Every empire uses a different class of primary weapon, and each primary weapon class has a number of types available.

NOTE

The statistics shown for each weapon type are for general comparative purposes only. Weapon ranges, power consumption, damage, and firing rate vary from weapon to weapon. Just because two weapons have a range of "average" doesn't mean that both have exactly the same range—just that their performance characteristics are similar. The best way to discover weapon abilities is to experiment with them in battle.

Federation Primary Weapons (Phasers)

Phasers have been the primary weapons of Federation starships since the beginning of the 23rd century (see Figure 2.1). Phasers—acronym for PHASed Energy Rectification—emit a coherent beam of light that is capable of effects ranging from a mild stun to the complete dissolution of matter at the sub-atomic level.

Standard 24th century phaser banks are available in six basic types:

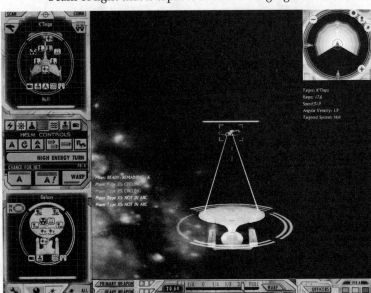

 Type-IX: These are low-powered, short-range phaser banks that are usually mounted on shuttles and smaller starships.

 Type-X: Standard phaser banks with medium-power yield and long range, type-X phasers are the most common primary weapons on Federation vessels.

Type-XI: A high-power upgrade to the type-X, these phasers have added punch over type-X, but only slightly better range.

Figure 2.1 Type-X phasers are the standard on most Federation starships, including Galaxy-class vessels.

Type-XII: The most powerful phaser bank that can be mounted on a starship, the type-XII has a high damage yield and a range that matches that of the type-X.

 Type-XIII: These phaser banks, found only on large, stationary Federation installations such as starbases, have a slightly longer range and higher power than any starship phaser.

Pulse Phasers: This weapon was developed in conjunction with the Federation's *Defiant* project. This weapon uses a different emitter type that releases phaser energy in rapid, layered pulses (see Figure 2.2). The damage potential of pulse phasers is equal to that of type-X standard phasers, and the nature of phaser pulses makes it possible for this weapon to occasionally penetrate shielding. The drawback is limited range (just slightly better than that of type-IX phasers) and relatively high power requirements.

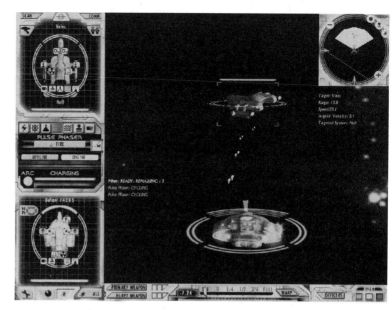

Figure 2.2 The *USS Defiant* was the first Federation starship equipped with pulse phasers.

The statistics for all phaser weapons are listed in Table 2.1.

PHASER TYPE	RANGE	DAMAGE	ENERGY CONSUMPTION	RATE OF FIRE
IXS	Very Short	Light	Very Low	Average
IXF	Very Short	Very Light	Very Low	Very Fast
XS	Short	Light	Low	Average
XF	Short	Light	Low	Very Fast
XIS	Average	Medium	Medium	Average
XIF	Average	Light	Low	Very Fast
XIIS	Long	Heavy	High	Average
XIIF	Long	Medium	High	Very Fast
XIIIS	Very Long	Heavy	Very High	Average
XIIIF	Very Long	Heavy	Very High	Very Fast
Pulse	Short	Medium	Low	Average

Table 2.1 Phaser Statistics

With the exception of pulse phasers, all primary weapon types are available in two models: standard (S) and fast (F). The speeds refer to the weapon's firing rate. Fast weapons cycle about twice as fast on average as slow weapons. As you can see from the statistics in Tables 2.1–2.3, standard weapons inflict more damage per shot than their fast counterparts, however, fast weapons potentially inflict more damage over time than slow phasers. For example, the type-XS phaser inflicts about one-third more damage per hit than type-XF, but since the XF fires twice for every one time the XS fires, the potential damage for an XF phaser over the same period is about one-third higher than for the XS. If you're fighting targets that you can keep in your sights for extended periods, it pays to upgrade to fast weapons.

Klingon and Romulan Primary Weapons (Disruptors)

Disruptors, like phasers, are directed-energy weapons. Klingon disruptors fire in a series of rapid pulses (see Figure 2.3), while the Romulan versions fire continuous beams. That said, the end result is very similar to that of a phaser barrage.

There are five disruptor bank models in common use in the 24th century:

 Type-I: These low-yield weapons are mounted almost exclusively on shuttlecraft and small starships.

 Type-II: With longer range and higher firepower than type-I units, type-II disruptors are standard-issue on most mid-size vessels.

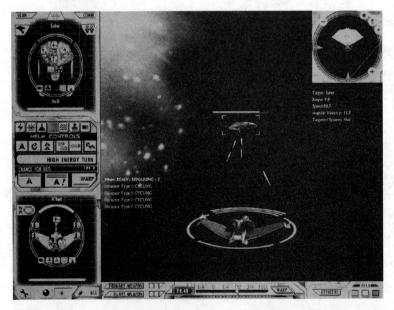

 Type-III: These disruptors have more raw firepower than type-II banks, but only slightly more range.

 Type-IV: The state-of-the-art type-IV disruptors are the most powerful disruptors available for starship use. Their range and firepower are greater than those of type-III units.

 Type-V: Too bulky to be mounted on starships, type-V disruptors are standard weaponry on Klingon and Romulan bases.

Figure 2.3 Disruptors are the Klingon and Romulan primary weapons of choice.

Unlike most weapons in *SFC3*, two major empires—Klingon and Romulan—use disruptors. Although both versions use similar technology, there are functional differences.

Klingon disruptors have slightly less firepower than their Romulan counterparts, but faster firing rates and lower power consumption. Table 2.2 shows the statistics for Klingon disruptors.

DISRUPTOR TYPE	RANGE	DAMAGE	ENERGY CONSUMPTION	RATE OF FIRE
I	Very Short	Light	Very Low	Average
IF	Very Short	Very Light	Very Low	Very Fast
II	Short	Light	Low	Average
IIF	Short	Light	Low	Very Fast
III	Average	Medium	Medium	Average
IIIF	Average	Light	Medium	Very Fast
IV	Long	Heavy	High	Average
IVF	Long	Medium	High	Very Fast
V	Very Long	Heavy	Very High	Average
VF	Very Long	Heavy	Very High	Very Fast

Table 2.2 Klingon Disruptor Statistics

Romulan disruptors sacrifice some of the speed and power efficiency of the Klingon versions for more firepower (see Table 2.3).

DISRUPTOR TYPE	RANGE	DAMAGE	ENERGY CONSUMPTION	RATE OF FIRE
R-I	Very Short	Light	Very Low	Slow
R-IF	Very Short	Light	Very Low	Fast
R-II	Short	Medium	Low	Slow
R-IIF	Short	Light	Low	Fast
R-III	Average	Heavy	Medium	Slow
R-IIIF	Average	Medium	Medium	Fast
R-IV	Long	Heavy	Very High	Slow
R-IVF	Long	Medium	Very High	Fast
R-V	Very Long	Very Heavy	Very High	Slow
R-VF	Very Long	Heavy	Very High	Fast

Table 2.3 Romulan Disruptor Statistics

Borg Primary Weapons (Cutting Beams)

Borg cutting beams are among the most powerful primary weapons in the game. They average better firepower across the board than comparable phasers and disruptors, and heavy cutting beams have longer range than any primary weapon available for starship use (see Figure 2.4).

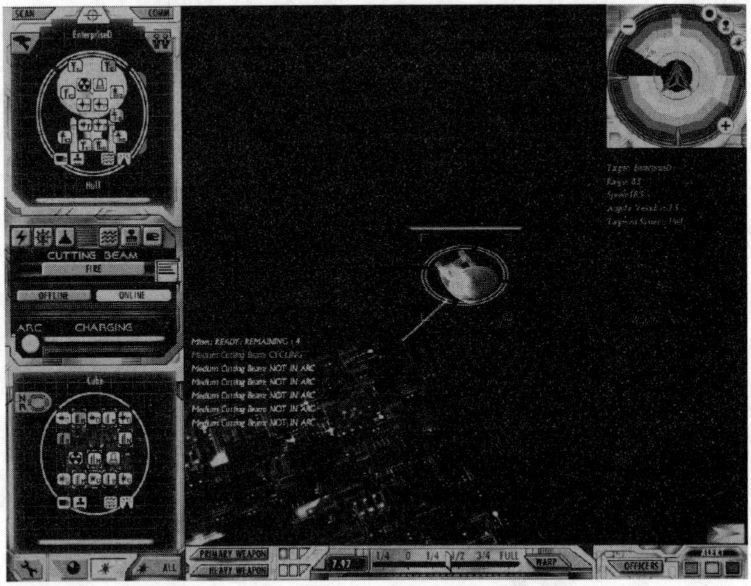

There are three cutting beam types:

 Light Cutting Beam: The least powerful cutting beam is found on smaller Borg vessels. The range is equivalent to that of smaller phasers and disruptors.

 Medium Cutting Beam: The standard Borg primary weapon, medium cutting beams inflict damage roughly equivalent to that of type-XI phasers or Klingon type-III disruptors.

 Heavy Cutting Beam: The Borg have the distinction of being the only empire that can mount their heaviest weapon on starships as well as bases. Luckily, heavy cutting beams are slightly less powerful than the heaviest phasers and disruptors.

Figure 2.4 Borg heavy cutting beams have the longest range of any ship-mounted primary weapon.

The statistics for Borg cutting beams are shown in Table 2.4.

BEAM TYPE	RANGE	DAMAGE	ENERGY CONSUMPTION	RATE OF FIRE
Light	Very Short	Light	Very Low	Average
Light-Fast	Very Short	Light	Very Low	Very Fast
Medium	Average	Medium	Low	Average
Medium-Fast	Average	Light	Low	Very Fast
Heavy	Long	Heavy	Very High	Average
Heavy-Fast	Long	Heavy	Very High	Very Fast

Table 2.4 Borg Cutting Beam Statistics

HEAVY WEAPONS

Heavy weapons are your ship's "glamour" weapons. They generally have greater range and better power-to-damage ratios than primary weapons, but pay for their power with slow cycle times and limited firing arcs.

Heavy weapons are often used to weaken enemy shields at long range in preparation for close-range assault with primary weapons. Many starship designs feature heavy weapons with aft firing arcs, which act as powerful deterrents to pursuing enemy vessels.

Like primary weapons, every empire has one or more heavy weapons that they use almost exclusively, so heavy weapon descriptions are categorized by empire. The tachyon pulse heavy beam weapon and antimatter mine layers are available to all empires, and so are covered separately at the end of the chapter.

Federation Heavy Weapons

 Photon torpedoes are solid projectiles that travel at high speed under their own power. They are equipped with antimatter warheads that detonate on impact, or in the case of the Federation version, in close proximity to their target (see Figure 2.5).

 Quantum torpedoes were developed in the late-2360s and are used exclusively by the Federation (see Figure 2.6). They are similar to photon torpedoes, but have greater range and explosive force. Like Federation photon torpedoes, quantum torpedoes can be set for proximity explosions.

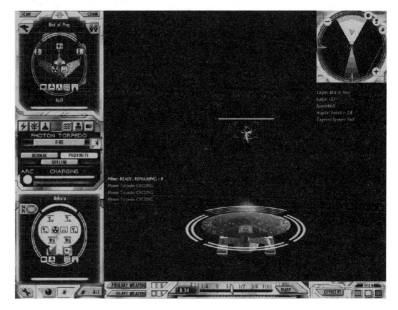

Figure 2.5 Both Klingon and Federation starships make wide use of photon torpedoes.

Photon and quantum torpedoes require a great deal of energy but provide a good damage yield for the expenditure. Their slow rates of fire are on par with other heavy weapons.

NOTE

Torpedoes of all types are unique in that they are the only weapons that can be used at warp speed. This allows you to make fast-pass hit-and-run attacks on enemy ships without dropping out of warp.

Federation heavy weapon statistics are shown in Table 2.5.

NOTE

The Federation is at a slight disadvantage when it comes to heavy weapons. Unlike the other empires, they have no exclusive heavy beam weapon. Federation vessels can, however, use the powerful tachyon pulse. (See the "Tachyon Pulse" section later in this chapter for details.)

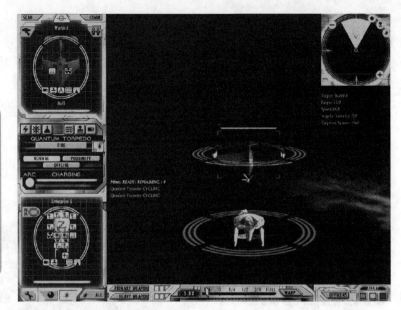

Figure 2.6 Quantum torpedoes are standard issue on state-of-the-art Federation starships such as the new Sovereign-class vessels.

WEAPON	RANGE	DAMAGE	ENERGY CONSUMPTION	RATE OF FIRE
Photon Torpedo	Long	Medium[1]	Medium	Slow
Quantum Torpedo	Very Long	Heavy[1]	High	Slow

1. Proximity blast yields 50% of normal damage.

Table 2.5 Federation Heavy Weapon Statistics

Klingon Heavy Weapons

Like Federation vessels, the most common heavy weapons on Klingon starships are photon torpedoes. Klingon photon torpedoes are similar in operation to their Federation counterparts, but have slightly less range and firepower, and cannot be armed for proximity detonation. They make up for these deficits by drawing less power than the Federation version.

Polaron torpedoes are advanced Klingon weapons that will make you think twice about using photons. They have a range advantage, but that isn't their best feature. Unlike most weapons, some polaron torpedo damage penetrates shielding, delivering destructive energy directly to the target's hull (see Figure 2.7). The combination of range and shield penetration makes polaron torpedoes ideal for attacks on heavily shielded targets such as starbases.

In addition to torpedoes, the Klingons have a heavy beam weapon: the ion cannon. This weapon is extremely powerful: similar to a tachyon pulse (which is described later in this chapter), but with no warp-dampening effects (see Figure 2.8). Because the difference in prestige is negligible between the ion cannon and the tachyon pulse, go for the tachyon pulse if you can afford it.

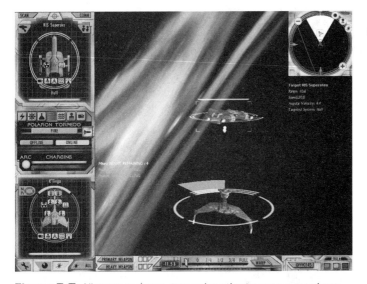

Klingon heavy weapon
statistics are shown in Table 2.6.

NOTE

Because polaron torpedoes don't have as great an effect on shields, ships equipped with these weapons can't use the standard attack pattern of using heavy weapons to weaken shields. If you must take out a target's shields, arm your ship with a combination of polaron torpedoes and other heavy weapon types.

Figure 2.7 Klingon polaron torpedoes have a range advantage over standard photon torpedoes—plus the ability to penetrate shields.

WEAPON	RANGE	DAMAGE	ENERGY CONSUMPTION	RATE OF FIRE
Photon Torpedo (Klingon)	Long	Light	Low	Average
Polaron Torpedo	Very Long	Heavy	High	Slow
Ion Cannon	Average	Heavy	Medium	Slow

Table 2.6 Klingon Heavy Weapon Statistics

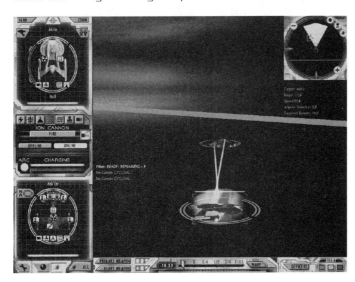

Figure 2.8 Ion cannons combine the punch of a powerful torpedo with the accuracy of a beam weapon.

Romulan Heavy Weapons

Plasma torpedoes are the Romulan heavy weapons of choice (see Figure 2.9). There are three varieties available:

 Light plasma torpedoes: These weapons are similar in performance to Klingon photon torpedoes but have slightly less range than most torpedo weapons.

 Medium plasma torpedoes: More powerful than their light counterparts, these weapons consume more energy but yield higher damage.

 Heavy plasma torpedoes: The range and damage yield of heavy plasma torpedoes make them among the most formidable weapons in the game.

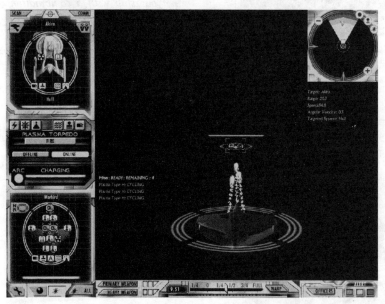

Figure 2.9 The range and power of Romulan heavy plasma torpedoes rival any weapon—heavy or otherwise—in the game.

Light plasma torpedoes aside, the drawback of these weapons is their power consumption. Medium and heavy plasma torpedoes draw a great deal of power. This puts Romulan ships at something of a disadvantage when their warp engines are damaged or power is diverted to other systems. Plasma torpedoes also have a very slow recharge rate—but they're worth the wait.

 The Romulan heavy beam weapon, the myotronic beam, has the ability to "stun" enemy weapon systems for a short time, preventing them from firing (see Figure 2.10). This ability makes myotronic beams very useful, especially in team assaults and base attack missions, where neutralizing enemy fire, even momentarily, makes the battle much easier.

Romulan heavy weapon stats are shown in Table 2.7.

NOTE

Star Fleet Command *veterans should note that plasma torpedoes perform differently in SFC3. They are now direct-fire weapons and do not lose damage potential over distance. You cannot outrun them, nor can you shoot them with phasers to reduce their damage potential.*

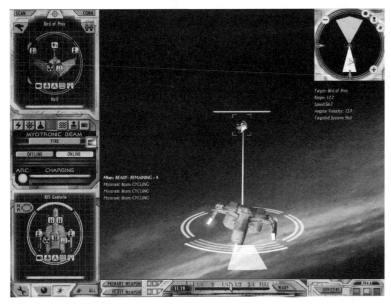

Figure 2.10 The weapon-stunning effect of myotronic beams gives you extra time to recharge your weapons and come around for another pass.

WEAPON	RANGE	DAMAGE	ENERGY CONSUMPTION	RATE OF FIRE
Light Plasma Torpedo	Average	Heavy	Low	Very Slow
Medium Plasma Torpedo	Long	Very Heavy	Medium	Very Slow
Heavy Plasma Torpedo	Very Long	Very Heavy	Very High	Very Slow
Myotronic Beam	Average	Medium	Medium	Average

Table 2.7 Romulan Heavy Weapon Statistics

Borg Heavy Weapons

Borg primary weapons have statistics that are generally similar to those of other empires. The Borg advantage is versatility: most of their ships can fire heavy weapons in every conceivable direction rather than just fore and aft. This is another reason not to mess with the Borg if you can help it.

 The heavy weapons most commonly found on Borg vessels are gravimetric torpedoes (see Figure 2.11). They are similar in performance to Federation photon torpedoes, but yield more damage.

 The shield inversion beam is an interesting weapon. It delivers its damage in a unique manner. Instead of hitting a single shield, the shield inversion beam hits all shields simultaneously, distributing its damage evenly (see Figure 2.12).

Although this is a seemingly powerful trait, it also limits the effectiveness of the weapon. To have a significant impact in the short term, several shield inversion beams must be brought to bear simultaneously and repeatedly. The design of most Borg vessels precludes this possibility. The shield inversion beam is an interesting novelty weapon, but the tachyon pulse (which is available to the Borg as well as all other empires) is a better deal if you have the prestige to spare.

Borg heavy weapon statistics are shown in Table 2.8.

Figure 2.11 Borg gravimetric torpedoes are like medium plasma torpedoes with a longer range and a faster firing rate.

WEAPON	RANGE	DAMAGE	ENERGY CONSUMPTION	RATE OF FIRE
Gravimetric Torpedo	Long	Heavy	Medium	Slow
Shield Inversion Beam	Average	Medium	Medium	Average

Table 2.8 Borg Heavy Weapon Statistics

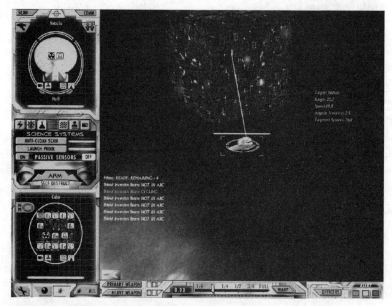

Figure 2.12 Your target's heading is irrelevant. Borg shield-inversion beams hit every shield at once.

Tachyon Pulse

The tachyon pulse is a universal beam weapon. Every empire can use it. This weapon inflicts damage similar to that of a Federation quantum torpedo at a similar energy cost but at a slower rate of fire (see Figure 2.13). The weapon also has an interesting side effect. It creates a subspace distortion field that prevents the target vessel from using its warp drive for a short time. This weapon is the ideal foil to enemies who like to use short warp jumps to get the drop on you.

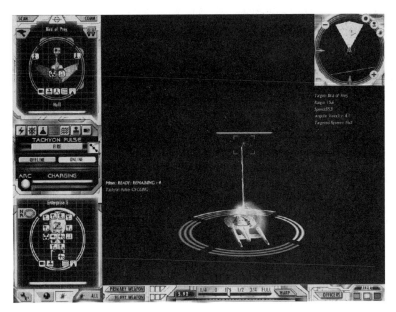

Figure 2.13 The tachyon pulse is a powerful heavy weapon that is available to all empires.

 The only downside to this weapon is that, like all other heavy beam weapons, its range is shorter than that of most torpedoes. This puts you at a range disadvantage against most ships sporting torpedoes as heavy weapons.

Tachyon pulse statistics are shown in Table 2.9.

WEAPON	RANGE	DAMAGE	ENERGY CONSUMPTION	RATE OF FIRE
Tachyon Pulse	Short	Medium	Medium	Slow

Table 2.9 Tachyon Pulse Statistics

Mines

Mine warfare is a universal concept. Every starship is equipped with a minelayer that can drop standard mines. When you drop a mine and move out of range, the mine goes active (changes from green to red). Any ship that moves into the mine's detection range at this point (enemy or otherwise) detonates the mine (see Figure 2.14).

In addition to standard mines, all empires can add an antimatter minelayer to any starship. The prestige cost is relatively high considering the limited utility of this weapon, but the high damage yield, quick cycle rate, and nearly non-existent energy cost makes it tempting to give this weapon a try. The presence of an antimatter minelayer automatically changes all standard mines aboard (and those you buy in the supply dock) to antimatter mines, but does not increase the maximum number of mines the ship can carry. Therefore, adding multiple antimatter minelayers to your ship increases the number of mines you can deploy in a given time period, but also depletes your mine supply faster. Note that you can always tell the difference between deployed antimatter and standard mines: antimatter mines are blue when active.

The statistics for mines are shown in Table 2.10.

Figure 2.14 Enemy mine.

WEAPON	RANGE	DAMAGE	ENERGY CONSUMPTION	RATE OF FIRE
Standard Mine	Special	Medium	Low	Average
Antimatter Minelayer	Special	Very Heavy	Low	Average

Table 2.10 Mine Statistics

TIP

An interesting tactic you might want to try in a team-based game or fleet scenario is to equip one ship as a minelayer—nothing but antimatter minelayers as heavy weapons. This ship can lay a field of antimatter mines as a surprise for the enemy fleet. Such a ship can also lay a minefield to protect a starbase in a starbase defense mission. Mines last only a limited time before exploding, though, so you have to lure your enemy in close before the mines expire.

3

Advanced Tactical Training

Now that you've got the basics of starship control down pat and you're familiar with the weapon systems with which your ship is equipped, it's time to put that knowledge to use in combat. Many hours of practical experience are required to master the intricacies of basic starship combat, and you need more time still before you become proficient at such advanced techniques as using tractor beams and boarding parties in a battle.

In this chapter, we'll start by teaching you some general combat techniques and skills that apply to almost any tactical situation. From there, we'll progress to advanced skills and tactics that help you to cope with both spatial conditions and specific combat situations you might encounter.

GENERAL COMBAT TACTICS

"I am a graduate of Starfleet Academy. I know many things."—Worf

There are a few general combat tactics that are the foundation for successful commanders. If you get a good grasp of these general principles, you should be prepared for most tactical situations.

Shields—Yours and Theirs

Shield management in combat is among the most useful skills you can master. This goes beyond the simple energy allocation techniques described in Chapter 1. Combat shield tactics involve a combination of maneuvering and selective shield reinforcement (see Figure 3.1).

Figure 3.1 Keeping a strong shield between you and the enemy improves your chances for survival.

When entering combat range, assess your targets and their respective firepower and range. Reinforce the shield facing the most powerful enemy—that doesn't necessarily mean the enemy you're currently targeting. If you're in a battle that strays close to an enemy base or other fixed facility, or you're concentrating on one of several powerful starships in a group, you must decide which target can deal the most damage at the current range and put your reinforcement between you and that target (see Figure 3.2).

As you alter your course, move your shield reinforcement to compensate for your change in position. Remember that there is a slight delay when you change reinforcement from shield to shield, so plan ahead so you're always reinforced where you need it most.

When you've taken lots of damage to a single shield, your reinforcement priorities change. After taking damage, always reinforce the weakest shield. Always endeavor to keep your weakest shields away from enemy targets until your shields have time to regenerate. Don't hesitate to move out of their weapon range to allow your shields to recuperate if you've sustained heavy damage.

When attacking an enemy target, always target its weakest shield. The weaker the shield, the faster you can break through and damage the ship. This is especially important when you're captaining a ship with relatively weak weapons. Don't waste your shots on strong or reinforced shields (see Figure 3.3).

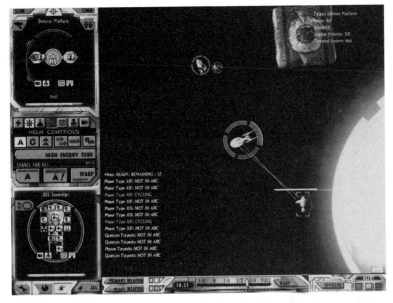

Figure 3.2 Reinforce the shield that lies between you and the local target with the most potential firepower.

The *Top Gun* Maneuver

Reverse thrust is a new feature in *SFC3*, and it provides a new way to shake pursuers and put your ship in a favorable offensive position in one simple maneuver.

When you have an enemy ship on your tail and you can't shake it or bring your forward weapons to bear because the enemy is too fast or maneuverable, throw your ship into reverse. Your sudden deceleration often takes your pursuer by surprise, causing them to fly right past you and into your forward firing arc before they can alter course. This is particularly effective in a high-speed pursuit, when maneuvering is difficult.

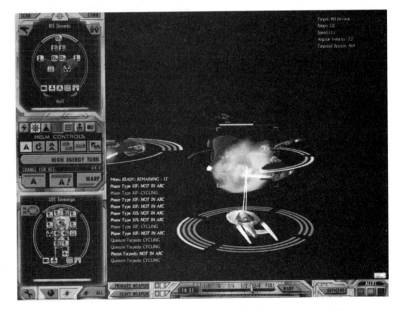

Figure 3.3 Make the most of your attacks by concentrating on the enemy's weakest shield.

If all goes well, you can shake pursuit and "go to guns" on the target's rear simultaneously.

Grouping Weapons

You can link weapons together so that you can fire them in selected groups. Group weapons by holding down the Ctrl key and clicking the weapons you want to fire, then clicking the Fire button (or pressing Z).

You can also make groupings permanent by selecting all of the weapons you want to group, holding down the Ctrl key, and pressing a number key. You can map one grouping to each number key, and thereafter you simply have to press the corresponding number to activate the mapped weapon group.

Weapon grouping is a great way to avoid wasting firepower. You fire only the weapons you need at any given time. For example, group a couple of weak phasers or disruptors and keep them in reserve for dealing with enemy shuttlecraft.

TIP

If you equip your ship with antimatter minelayers, always group the minelayers separately from the other weapons. You don't want to be dropping mines every time you fire your forward weapons!

The Alpha-Strike

The most widely practiced offensive tactic is the "alpha-strike," by which you move into weapon range with the enemy in your forward sights and cut loose with every facing weapon simultaneously (see Figure 3.4).

Alpha-strike combat is popular with human and AI captains alike, and with good reason: nothing opens a hole in an enemy's shields faster than unloading with everything you've got. Alpha-striking ensures that all of your weapons hit a single shield, whereas selective firing requires skillful maneuvering in some cases to maintain focus on one shield.

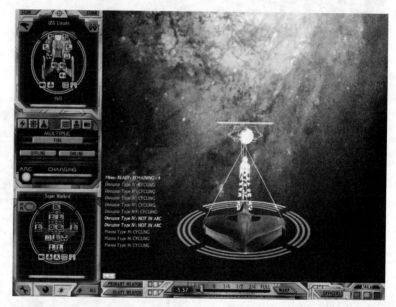

Figure 3.4 Nothing is more satisfying than an effective alpha-strike.

Don't Forget
Your Other Weapons

The massive power of the alpha-strike often blinds you to the full offensive capability of your ship. Some ships don't have weapons that reach beyond the forward firing arc, but if your ship does, make use of those lateral and aft weapons whenever possible.

If you have port and starboard weapons with wide firing arcs, all it takes is slight course adjustments to port and starboard to bring these weapons into play. You can do this without altering your course significantly if you're trying to keep the enemy in your sights for repeated alpha-strikes.

If your side weapon arcs aren't generous enough to permit the aforementioned tactic, you can bring your lateral weapons into play by changing course. Against slow-moving or stationary targets, you can more or less just sit in place and spin to port or starboard to zap the enemy (see Figure 3.5). Continue your turn to fire your aft weapons if you've got them. This is a great tactic for ships with well-balanced firepower all the way around (such as Klingon K'Tinga-class vessels.)

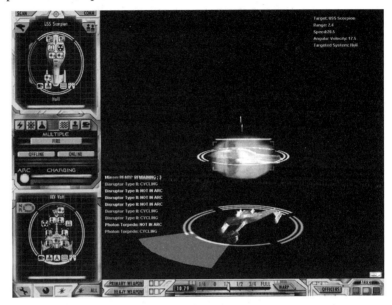

Figure 3.5 The "Star Castle" technique—spinning in place at low speeds—lets you bring all your weapons to bear.

Against faster targets, you can usually bring at least one lateral battery into play by veering off course after you deliver your main forward weapon strike.

Always attempt to incorporate a parting side and/or aft shot into every attack run. After your forward weapons have (hopefully) weakened the target's shields, the extra blast from your side weapons is a great way to score some internal damage before the target's shields regenerate.

Targeting Individual Systems

By default, damage that penetrates an enemy's shields is applied to the ship's hull. You can, however, target individual enemy systems.

To target a particular enemy system, click it on the Target Data display (see Figure 3.6). The name of the targeted system appears on both the Target Data display and in the enemy data readout on the Main View screen. All damage that gets past the shields is applied specifically to that system.

The most useful subsystems to target are those that put your enemy at a significant disadvantage. Weapons are the obvious choices, but taking out a single weapon system seldom makes much of a difference in ship performance. Engine systems are better targets. Damaging the enemy's warp drive, for example, limits the amount of power they can allocate not only to weapon systems but also to shields.

Do not attempt this tactic unless your tactical officer is an expert or veteran in subsystem targeting. If you miss, damage that could have been applied to the target's hull is wasted.

Figure 3.6 You can take out a specific target system by selecting it on the Target Data display.

TIP

Rather than targeting specific systems, you might consider beaming your marines to the enemy ship for a hit-and-run raid. That way, you inflict more damage with your weapons fire and you still have a chance of knocking out the specific system you want eliminated.

Fleet Tactics

When there are ships fighting on your side under your command—that is, the friendly ships are subordinate to you or were captured by you—you can give them a series of simple commands via your communications system:

Set Target: Tells your allies whom to attack. You can order them to target at will (choose their own targets), or attack or capture the target you're currently locked onto.

Set Formation: Orders allied ships to move into a formation of your choice.

Move To: Orders the ships to move to a location that you specify.

Cloak/Decloak: Tells allied ships to engage or disengage their cloaking devices (if they're so equipped).

Disengage: Orders the ships to leave the sector.

NOTE

Starfleet Command veterans should note that you can no longer take direct command of other ships in your armada, nor do you jump to another vessel in the fleet if yours is destroyed.

You can give orders to all of the subordinate ships in your fleet simultaneously or individually. If you give the orders simultaneously, only the ships that are able to comply with the command do so.

WARP DRIVE IN COMBAT

There are a lot of new features in *SFC3*, but of all the upgrades to the game, nothing changes combat tactics as much as the addition of warp drive. The ability to jump to trans-light speed in combat not only lets you turn tail and run when things get out of hand, it also creates the opportunity for some interesting combat strategies.

Warp Jumping

The most basic warp drive combat maneuver is the warp jump. When you're up against an enemy ship that is faster or more maneuverable than yours, it's difficult to execute some of the most basic combat tactics in the game, such as holding position off a single enemy quarter so that you can deliver all damage to one shield and bringing your ship's most powerful firing arcs to bear after your weapons recharge.

By using a one- or two-second warp jump, you can gain distance on the enemy target and give yourself enough room to come around for another pass. When trying to gain distance for a weapons run, warp away from the target at a 45-degree angle to the target's course in a direction that keeps the enemy's weakest shield toward you. After you're out of weapon range, swing around and make your run (see Figure 3.7).

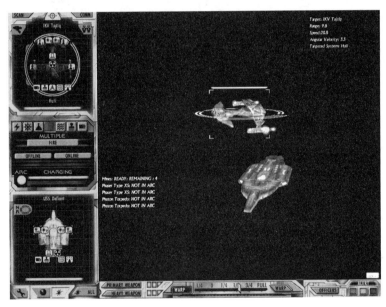

Figure 3.7 Warp jumps allow you to gain distance to recharge your weapons and come around for another pass.

Strafing Runs

Primary weapons are inactive while warp drive is engaged, but most heavy weapons—torpedoes, for example—are fully operational at warp velocities. This allows you to perform strafing runs on targets.

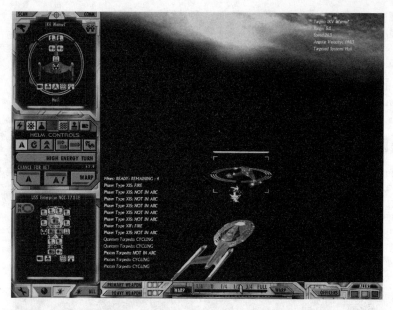

Point your ship at the target vessel and engage your warp drive. When you enter firing range, loose a heavy weapon salvo and continue warping past the target (see Figure 3.8). If your ship has rear-firing heavy weapons, hit the enemy again from the opposite side as you pass.

Remember, you're vulnerable to enemy weapons fire when you're at warp, so plan your strafing runs so that your approach and retreat takes you through the enemy's weakest firing arcs. On most targets, your best bet is to strafe from port to starboard (or vice versa), where most ships have minimal weaponry.

Figure 3.8 *Delivering a spread of quantum torpedoes at warp speed.*

FUN WITH MINES

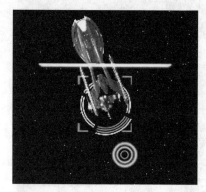

One of the problems with mine warfare is that by the time you are out of range and the mine you drop has armed itself, the enemy you're trying to hit with the mine is also out of range.

Warp drive opens up a whole new mine-laying strategy. When you drop a mine, make a quick warp jump away from the scene and the mine arms itself almost instantly. This increases the chance of the mine delivering damage before your enemy can retreat to a safe distance.

A bolder strategy uses warp drive to drop mines directly in your opponent's path. Set yourself up so that you're facing your enemy head-on or you're perpendicular to the enemy's course and slightly ahead of the target vessel. Plot your warp jump so that you intersect the target's course just slightly ahead of its position (see Figure 3.9). When you're directly in the enemy's path, drop out of warp, drop a mine, and re-engage your warp drive to flee the scene. If you time this maneuver correctly, your enemy won't have time to react and change course before the mine arms itself and explodes (see Figure 3.10).

Figure 3.9 *Drop out of warp, drop a mine directly in your enemy's path, and warp out immediately.*

Figure 3.10 *If you time your bombing run correctly, the mine arms itself and explodes before your target can change course.*

34

Chapter 3: Advanced Tactical Training

Warp-speed bombing runs are extremely dangerous because they expose your unshielded ship to your enemy's forward batteries for several seconds. To avoid the possibility of heavy damage to your ship, time your bombing runs to coincide with the recharging of your target's forward weapons.

TIP

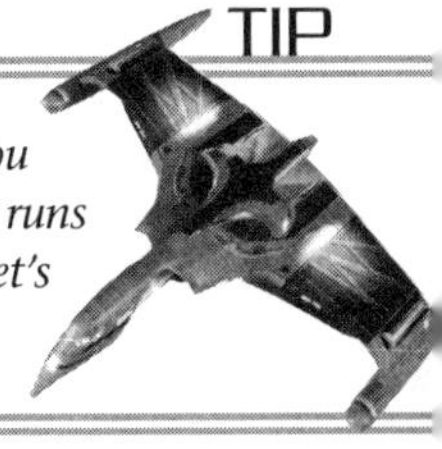

If you choose a head-on course, you can combine strafing and bombing runs to absolutely decimate your target's forward shields.

SHUTTLECRAFT

In most engagements, it's you versus the galaxy. The biggest problem in such a scenario is that there are no other targets to draw enemy fire away from your ship. This is particularly troublesome when you're facing multiple enemies.

Shuttlecraft draw enemy fire and provide a little extra firepower of their own to supplement your attacks. Shuttle weapons are short range and weak, but they can do some significant damage if you get the enemy's shields down (see Figure 3.11).

Shuttlecraft have three operational modes:

Attack: The shuttlecraft moves in to close range and aggressively engages enemy targets. Attack shuttles don't usually last long (unless they're lucky), but they have the best chance of inflicting significant damage to their targets.

Snipe: The shuttlecraft engages enemy targets from a distance while taking evasive action. This increases the shuttle's life expectancy, but inflicts less damage to enemy targets.

Defend: The shuttlecraft sticks close to your ship and engages targets only when they become a direct threat.

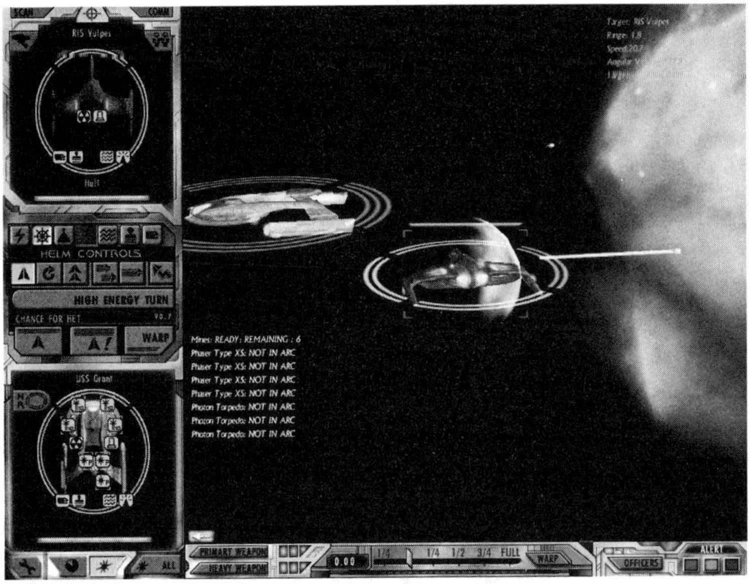

Figure 3.11 Deploy shuttlecraft to add to your firepower.

When you successfully complete a mission, surviving shuttlecraft are automatically recovered. If you're forced to disengage before the battle is over, you must order the shuttlecraft to return or else you lose them when you leave the sector.

Shuttlecraft are an effective way to increase your firepower and draw away enemy firepower that might otherwise be directed at you. They're also cheap to replace, so stock up every time you visit a base. (Just try not to think about the poor red-shirted crewmen who sacrifice their lives as shuttle pilots.)

THE CLOAKING DEVICE

The cloaking device is a great equalizer. A small vessel that can cloak can effectively take on much larger targets and still survive—and even emerge victorious (see Figure 3.12).

Effective cloaking tactics require some practice, but the skills are relatively easy to master. The basic sequence for cloaked combat is as follows:

1. **Cloak immediately on entering the sector.** If you cloak before the enemy detects you, you can easily get the drop on them.

2. **Remain cloaked until all of your weapons are charged.**

3. **Approach the enemy target from a weak side.** Choose the weakest shield in an area of the ship that has little or no weapons coverage.

4. **Move in to close range, uncloak, and unleash an alpha-strike.** Cloaked combat is all about hitting hard and fast.

5. **Recloak and repeat.** After you expend your weapons, cloak immediately and start recharging for the next attack run.

The most important thing to remember when commanding a cloaked vessel is that there are the moments of vulnerability as you cloak and decloak. Make sure a minimum of enemy weapons can be brought to bear on you when you activate or deactivate your cloaking device. Don't just check your target's weapon arcs— check all around you. An enemy shuttle or another enemy ship might be sitting off to the side or behind you.

Figure 3.12 Strategic cloaking allows weak ships to prevail over much stronger vessels.

TIP

If possible, try to maintain your position off the same enemy shield or quarter between attack runs. If you successfully shadow the enemy, you can unleash strike after strike on the same shield with a minimum of maneuvering time, leaving the target shield little time to regenerate between attacks.

Anticloaking Tactics

Here are some combat tips for fighting cloaked ships:

Determine whether the ship is using cloak tactics. Human opponents almost always make use of their cloaking devices, but the AI doesn't. You might be able to use standard combat tactics.

Fire during the cloak/decloak period. If the enemy is visible, hold your fire until the target begins to cloak. Fire as soon as the target fades out. If the enemy is invisible, lock on and fire as soon as the decloaking message appears on your screen (see Figure 3.13). In both scenarios, you have a couple of seconds to score hits on an unshielded ship.

Use boarding parties. Since the enemy's shields are down and it cannot fire while cloaking and decloaking, you have an opportunity to beam over boarding parties to damage or capture the ship.

Warp away when your opponent cloaks. Unless you're relatively certain where your enemy will pop up next, use a brief warp jump to put some distance between you and the enemy's last known position.

Upgrade your computer. If you know you're going to be up against cloaking enemies, upgrade your ship's computer to a type that has an anticloak scan.

Fire probes. Firing a probe in the direction of the cloaked vessel might reveal its location.

There are a couple of cheats that allow you to see (but not target) a cloaked ship. When the enemy passes over your ship or through your turn indicator bar, you can see its "shadow" (see Figure 3.14). When a cloaked enemy is nearby, you can often track its position by making a series of wide turns and watching its shadow as it crosses the turn indicator.

TIP

When refitting a cloaked ship, pay particular attention to armor and weapon types. The heavier your armor, the better protected you are during those vulnerable cloaking and decloaking moments. Choose weapons for their raw damage potential rather than their recharge rate. The fire-and-hide tactics you use with a cloaked ship favor heavy alpha-strikes. Recharge rate is secondary, since you're hidden while your weapons cycle.

Figure 3.13 You can score some hull damage while a ship is cloaking or decloaking.

TIP

If you have a cloak, too, you can trick the AI into decloaking. Cloak and move slightly away from the enemy's last known position. Decloak momentarily when you gain some distance, then recloak. The enemy is often tricked into decloaking, thinking that there is a valid target available. This reveals its position, providing you with a target.

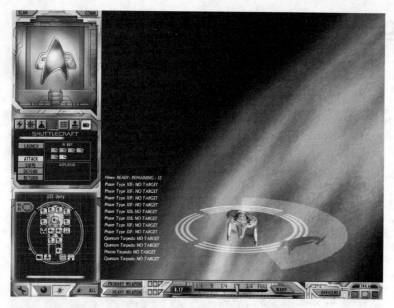

Figure 3.14 Track a cloaked ship's position by watching its shadow.

The same phenomenon occurs in a thick nebula. You can see a cloaked vessel's shadow as it passes over the areas of nebulosity. Keep your eyes open and, even though you can't lock on until the enemy decloaks, at least you know where they are most of the time.

TRACTOR BEAMS

Many players don't take advantage of tractor beams, but they can be extremely useful in certain situations. Tractor beam combat uses include

Preventing retreat: When an enemy is trying to make a run for it, use your tractors to keep the enemy close so that you can blast the vessel at your leisure.

Dragging or pushing enemies into harmful objects: Use your tractors to drag or push enemies into mines, asteroids, or planets (see Figure 3.15).

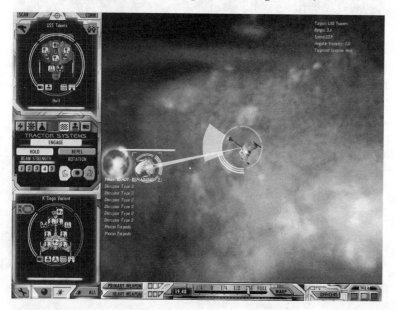

Exposing an enemy to all of your weapon arcs: Instead of turning your ship to take advantage of your lateral and aft firepower, tractor your target and rotate it around your ship, exposing it to each of your firing arcs in turn. (This is a great tactic when captaining a Borg Cube, which has trouble bringing all of its weapons to bear because of its lumbering nature.)

Tractor combat is tricky, and you should practice your tactics in single-player skirmishes before risking your ship in a campaign mission or trying these tricks against human opponents.

Figure 3.15 Tow targets into mines and other objects to inflict damage without firing a single shot.

Remember that when a ship is caught in a tractor beam, it can still rotate and fire even if it can't escape, so the target can hurt *you* while you're hurting it.

To escape from a tractor beam, turn away from the tractoring vessel and go to full impulse (you can't go to warp when you're caught in a tractor beam). If you start taking damage, it means that the enemy tractor is too powerful for you to escape. Immediately cut engine power and just roll with the punches until you can blast your way out of the predicament.

> **NOTE**
>
> *You cannot charge your tractor beam while traveling at warp speed, and going to warp when your tractor beam is charged discharges it. You must reactivate the tractor beam after you drop out of warp and recharge it from scratch.*

SEND IN THE MARINES

Mastering the deployment of marines can give you a significant edge in combat—especially if your security officer is an expert or veteran in all their skills. You can use your marines for two tasks: hit-and-run raids and Capture missions.

To initiate a marine mission, you must be within transporter range of the targeted enemy ship or installation. The success or failure of the mission depends on your security officer's experience level, the number of marines on the target compared to the number of marines you send over, and the experience of the target vessel or installation's security officer.

> **TIP**
>
> *Marine tactics require that you drop your shields while very close to an enemy target. Make sure the enemy cannot fire a significant number of weapons at your exposed side during marine transport.*

Hit-and-Run Raids

A hit-and-run raid targets specific systems on the enemy vessel or installation for destruction. You can select up to eight target systems at a time. The marines attack each system in turn in the order you selected them (see Figure 3.16).

By default, when you enter transporter range and the target's shields are down, the marines automatically start beaming over to attempt the raid. As long as systems remain in the queue, the marines continue to beam over and attempt to destroy the selected systems. If you're losing lots of marines and seeing no positive results, terminate the hit-and-run order by removing the targeted systems from the queue.

AI enemies often attempt hit-and-run raids on your ship. Make sure you don't expose a downed shield to an enemy vessel if you want to keep the boarding parties out.

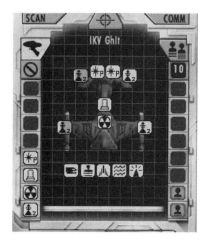

Figure 3.16 Attempting a series of hit-and-run raids.

Capturing Enemy Targets

Capturing a target is more difficult than making a simple hit-and-run raid, but the reward is substantially higher. If you're successful in capturing the target vessel, it fights *with* you rather than against you. This can be a major boon in missions where you're outnumbered and there are no friendly reinforcements in the area. In many core campaign missions, you also gain extra prestige for capturing ships and facilities rather than destroying them.

> **TIP**
>
> *If you enjoy employing marine tactics, equip your ship with the biggest transporter possible. The transporter's numeric designation (I–V) indicates the maximum number of marines it can transport each time you energize.*

To attempt a capture, move into transporter range on an unshielded side of the enemy vessel/installation and transport your marines over. The more marines you transport, the better your chances, so always use the All Marines option.

You can monitor the status of the capture by watching the progress bar on the Capture control panel (see Figure 3.17). When the bar goes completely blue, the target is captured. If progress is slow, transport more marines into the fray until the job is complete. Remember, the bigger the target, the more resistance your marines encounter.

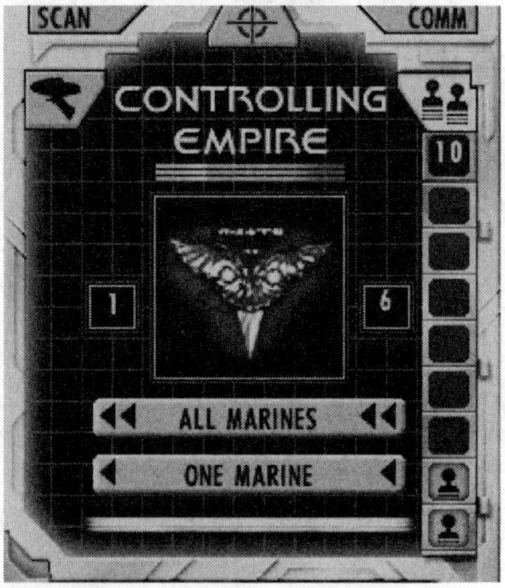

Figure 3.17 A battle rages on an enemy vessel as marines attempt to capture it.

DEALING WITH THE ENVIRONMENT

Although many missions take place in empty space, some sectors contain potentially hazardous phenomena. From time to time, you must deal with these special environments, some of which force you to rethink your tried and true combat tactics—and some of which inspire new ones.

The environments you have to deal with include

Asteroids and asteroid fields: Asteroid fields are floating masses of giant boulders, any of which can destroy your ship if you run into it. It's a good idea to zoom out and perhaps switch to Top-Down view when in an asteroid field so you can avoid accidentally flying into one. Keep your speed down and be prepared to make quick course corrections if need be.

Planets: Planets are huge and mostly harmless—that is, unless you run into one. When fighting near a planet, heed your collision warnings and zoom out or watch your passive sensor display so that you don't accidentally hit the surface.

Stars: Stars are quite dangerous at close range. When inside the star's corona, you take constant damage that quickly tears apart your shields and just as quickly tears apart your ship. There are tactical uses for this effect if you can lure an enemy into the danger zone, but unless you're certain of your own survival, steer clear of stars altogether.

Nebulae: These masses of gas, particles, and radiation are fairly common. They might cover an entire map or only certain sections of the sector. When inside a nebula, you cannot launch shuttles or drop mines. In addition, if you're cloaked, your shadow might be visible against the background radiation.

Black holes: Black holes are space hazards to be avoided at all costs. You can approach them safely up to a point, but beyond a certain range, their pull becomes so great that you cannot escape. Just how close you can get and still escape safely depends on how powerful your impulse engines are. When fighting in a black hole sector, be as vigilant as you would in an asteroid field to make sure you don't stray too close.

Dust clouds: Dust clouds are secondary phenomena that occur in asteroid fields, nebulae, and near some planets and stars. When you're in a dust cloud, keep your speed low. Beyond a certain speed, you begin to take damage in your forward quarter from the dust. This also applies to warp movement in a dust cloud (which is worse, since you don't have your shields to protect you).

NOTE

You cannot achieve sensor lock if a large environmental object— an asteroid or planet, for example— lies between you and your target, and you might lose lock-on if an object comes between you and a targeted ship.

4 The United Federation of Planets

The United Federation of Planets is one of the dominant empires in the Alpha and Beta Quadrants. Founded in 2161, the Federation comprised more than 150 worlds by 2373. The Federation's scientific, exploratory, and military organization, called Starfleet, has existed since the early 22nd century. Starfleet is headquartered on the planet Earth and has outposts and starbases throughout the Alpha and Beta Quadrants.

Prior to the Borg incursion of 2366, Federation starship designs tended toward science and defense roles. After the devastating battle at Wolf 359, which resulted in the loss of 39 starships and more than 11,000 lives, Starfleet ship designs became much more military. Newer Federation vessels feature advanced shield, armor, and weapon systems that were designed specifically to counter the Borg. Federation ships are thus now much more formidable enemies in battle.

With nine hull classes, the Federation fleet offers the greatest starship variety in the game. This chapter analyzes the strengths and weaknesses of the Federation vessels available to you and offers a tactical assessment of the abilities of each, along with upgrade recommendations for converting stock starships into top-notch warships.

For information on additional Federation vessels and installations, see Appendix A.

SABER-CLASS "FRIGATE"

"...to boldly go where no one has gone before."—Zefram Cochrane

NOTE

The point values shown for the default ships in this chapter and in Chapters 5, 6, and 7 reflect the value of the ship and its default systems and weapons alone. The officers and supplies (shuttles, marines, and mines) add to the final point value of the ship.

The Saber is the smallest hull class currently deployed by the Federation. Though the armament of this vessel is limited, its low mass and high speed make it ideal for scientific and patrol missions. This ship is easily the equal of a comparably equipped Klingon Bird of Prey or Romulan Talon-class vessel.

Saber-Class Frigate (Default Specifications)

Cost in Points	13,009
Total Mass	10,050
Total Impulse Power	425
Total Warp Power Usage	24.67 of 26
Top Speed	42.29
Maneuverability	1.09
Shields	4 F-Shield-II
Primary Weapons	3 Fore (3 Phaser IXS)
Heavy Weapons	1 Fore (Photon Torpedo)
Hull Systems	F-Tractor-I
	F-Armor-I
	F-Transporter-I
Bridge Systems	F-Computer-I
Engines	F-Thruster-I
	F-Impulse-I
	F-Warp-I
Shuttles (Default/Max)	1/2
Marines (Default/Max)	4/8
Mines (Default/Max)	2/8

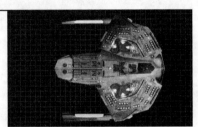

Saber-class frigate

There is some room for modification in the default Saber loadout. Suggested upgrades include

- Upgrade to Phaser-IXF on all attachment points.

- Upgrade the photon torpedo to a quantum torpedo.

The biggest weakness of the Saber is its lack of aft weapons. When captaining this vessel, use your superior speed and maneuverability to move out of range quickly between attack runs so that you can come around for another pass with minimum aft exposure to the enemy.

NORWAY-CLASS "DESTROYER"

The Norway-class destroyer is a state-of-the art ship that was designed shortly after the battle of Wolf 359 and entered active service several years later. The Norway class represents a significant improvement over previous Federation destroyer designs in terms of total warp power usage. A lone Norway-class vessel can hold its own against Klingon K'Vort and Romulan Falcon-class ships.

Norway-Class Destroyer (Default Specifications)

Cost in Points	16,959
Total Mass	13,325
Total Impulse Power	425
Total Warp Power Usage	34.67 of 36
Top Speed	31.89
Maneuverability	0.83
Shields	4 F-Shield-III
Primary Weapons	3 Fore (2 Phaser IXS, 1 empty)
Heavy Weapons	2 Fore (2 Photon Torpedoes)
	1 Aft (empty)
Hull Systems	F-Tractor-II
	F-Armor-I
	F-Transporter-I
Bridge Systems	F-Computer-I
Engines	F-Thruster-I
	F-Impulse-I
	F-Warp-III
Shuttles (Default/Max)	2/3
Marines (Default/Max)	5/10
Mines (Default/Max)	2/8

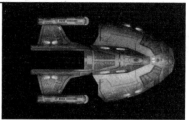

Norway-class destroyer

The default Norway loadout doesn't live up to the potential for this hull class. The following upgrades make this vessel much more formidable:

- Add a phaser XF to the empty attachment point and upgrade the existing phasers to XF.

- Move one of the forward photon torpedoes to the aft attachment point.

- Upgrade warp drive.

In its default configuration, the Norway suffers from an overall lack of primary firepower (compared with other ships of its class). This drawback makes it imperative that you use range to your advantage. Fire your photon torpedoes from long range to weaken the enemy's shields and make high-speed strafing runs with your phasers, retreating out of weapons range while you swing around for the next run.

DEFIANT-CLASS "LIGHT CRUISER"

Defiant-class light cruisers are warships, pure and simple. Tough, fast, and well armed, they were designed to go toe to toe with Borg vessels more than ten times their size. Although a default configuration Defiant isn't a match for a Borg ship more formidable than a Diamond or Pyramid, it can take on a Klingon K'Tinga or Romulan Shrike with little difficulty.

Defiant-Class Light Cruiser (Default Specifications)

Defiant-class light cruiser

Cost in Points	20,384
Total Mass	14,250
Total Impulse Power	510
Total Warp Power Usage	38.67 of 45
Top Speed	35.79
Maneuverability	0.89
Shields	4 F-Shield-III
Primary Weapons	3 Fore (2 Phaser XS, 1 empty)
Heavy Weapons	4 Fore (2 Photon Torpedoes, 2 empty)
Hull Systems	F-Tractor-II
	F-Armor-I
	F-Transporter-II
Bridge Systems	F-Computer-II
Engines	F-Thruster-II
	F-Impulse-II
	F-Warp-IV
Shuttles (Default/Max)	1/2
Marines (Default/Max)	6/12
Mines (Default/Max)	3/12

NOTE

Using the ship design/refit tool in Starfleet Command III, *you can recreate just about any* Star Trek *ship that you've seen on* Star Trek: Next Generation, Deep Space Nine, *and* Voyager. *See Chapter 8 for some design suggestions for famous Defiant-, Intrepid-, Galaxy- and Sovereign-class designs.*

The Defiant-class default configuration belies its potential. In its basic form, it has little advantage over the lighter Norway-class design. With a little work, however, this ship can become quite a formidable vessel:

- Upgrade the forward shield to type IV.

- Add a phaser XF to the empty attachment point.

- Upgrade the armor.

- Upgrade the impulse engines and thrusters.

Like the Saber-class frigate, the Defiant-class light cruiser suffers from a lack of aft armament, so use your maneuverability to minimize your rear exposure.

INTREPID-CLASS "LIGHT CRUISER"

Unlike Defiant-class vessels, the Federation's other light cruiser hull class, the Intrepid, is designed as a multi-role ship. A larger hull means more weapon and system capacity and, even in its default configuration, this ship carries more firepower than the smaller Defiant. The drawback is that the Intrepid-class ships are slower and less maneuverable than the Defiant-class. The Intrepid-class, properly equipped, can successfully hold its own against heavy cruisers.

Intrepid-Class Light Cruiser (Default Specifications)

Intrepid-class light cruiser

Cost in Points	24,609
Total Mass	19,700
Total Impulse Power	510
Total Warp Power Usage	50.67 of 53
Top Speed	25.89
Maneuverability	0.64
Shields	4 F-Shield-IV
Primary Weapons	2 Fore (2 Phaser XS)
	1 Port (empty)
	1 Starboard (empty)
	1 Aft (empty)
	1 360-degree (empty)
Heavy Weapons	2 Fore (2 Photon Torpedoes)
	2 Aft (1 Photon Torpedo, 1 empty)
Hull Systems	F-Tractor-III
	F-Armor-II
	F-Transporter-II
Bridge Systems	F-Computer-II
Engines	F-Thruster-II
	F-Impulse-II
	F-Warp-V
Shuttles (Default/Max)	1/3
Marines (Default/Max)	6/12
Mines (Default/Max)	3/12

> **TIP**
>
> *When you command a ship that has a 360-degree primary weapon attachment point, you should take advantage of it and mount the best weapon you can there. The most common drawbacks to ship designs are weapon blind spots. A 360-degree primary weapon (preferably one with a fast firing rate) is the ideal solution. It gives you weapon coverage in your weak quarters, and also bolsters your firepower in your strongest arcs.*

Intrepid-class light cruisers are well balanced when it comes to available weapon attachment points, but like most ships, the default design can use some tweaking. Refit suggestions include

- Upgrade the forward phasers to XF, and install a Phaser-XF in the 360-degree mount to provide port, starboard, and aft primary weapon coverage.

- Upgrade the armor.

- Upgrade the thrusters and impulse engines to improve maneuverability and speed.

The major problems that default Intrepid-class ships suffer are low maneuverability and speed compared with ships of similar size (the Klingon K'Tinga for example). Warp jumps are essential to your strategy in a stock Intrepid. Against a competent opponent, you have little hope of bringing your main weapons to bear after the first volley without first putting significant distance between you and your target.

AKIRA-CLASS "HEAVY CRUISER"

Akira-class heavy cruisers were introduced into the Federation fleet at about the same time as the Saber- and Norway-class vessels. This new generation ship is moving into the frontline fleet role previously held by Constitution- and Excelsior-class heavy cruisers. The highly maneuverable Akira is designed to be an even match for the new Klingon Fek'lhr and Romulan Hawk cruisers.

Akira-Class Heavy Cruiser (Default Specifications)

Cost in Points	30,409
Total Mass	23,950
Total Impulse Power	510
Total Warp Power Usage	62.67 of 72
Top Speed	21.29
Maneuverability	0.53
Shields	4 F-Shield-V
Primary Weapons	2 Fore (2 Phaser XS)
	2 Port (1 Phaser XS, 1 empty)
	2 Starboard (1 Phaser XS, 1 empty)
	1 360-degree (empty)
Heavy Weapons	2 Fore (2 Photon Torpedoes)
	2 Aft (1 Photon Torpedo, 1 empty)
Hull Systems	F-Tractor-III
	F-Armor-II
	F-Transporter-II
Bridge Systems	F-Computer-II
Engines	F-Thruster-II
	F-Impulse-II
	F-Warp-VI
Shuttles (Default/Max)	2/3
Marines (Default/Max)	10/20
Mines (Default/Max)	4/16

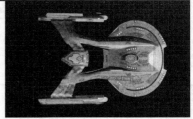

Akira-class heavy cruiser

Akira-class ships have a lot of improvement potential. To turn an Akira into a force to be reckoned with, try the following

• Upgrade the shields in the fore, port, and starboard quarters. (Upgrade the rear shields, too, if you can afford it.)

• Add a phaser XF to the 360-degree mount.

• Upgrade the thrusters and impulse engines.

Standard-configuration Akira-class ships suffer from the usual weakness: no aft primary weapons. Use your strong port and starboard primaries as you make course changes, and keep your forward shield reinforced and toward the enemy whenever possible.

EXCELSIOR-CLASS "HEAVY CRUISER"

The venerable Excelsior-class cruisers have served in Starfleet for more than 80 years with no major changes in design. This starship is proof that old design methods are still valid in the modern era. If properly equipped, the Excelsior-class vessels are arguably superior to Akira-class ships.

Excelsior-Class Heavy Cruiser (Default Specifications)

Cost in Points	29,409
Total Mass	26,400
Total Impulse Power	614
Total Warp Power Usage	58.67 of 66
Top Speed	23.26
Maneuverability	0.55
Shields	4 F-Shield-V
Primary Weapons	1 Fore (Phaser XS)
	2 Port (2 Phaser XS)
	2 Starboard (2 Phaser XS)
	1 Aft (empty)
Heavy Weapons	2 Fore (2 Photon Torpedoes)
	2 Aft (both empty)
Hull Systems	F-Tractor-III
	F-Armor-I
	F-Transporter-II
Bridge Systems	F-Computer-II
Engines	F-Thruster-III
	F-Impulse-III
	F-Warp-VI
Shuttles (Default/Max)	4/8
Marines (Default/Max)	12/24
Mines (Default/Max)	6/24

Excelsior-class heavy cruiser

Like most hull classes, the default Excelsior has some room for improvement. Suggestions include

• Upgrade the forward phaser to type-XF. (With only one forward phaser, a faster firing rate up front helps.)

• Add a type-XS phaser to the empty aft attachment point.

• Upgrade the thrusters and impulse engines.

In its default configuration, the Excelsior suffers from the usual lack of aft weapons, though the problem isn't quite as acute in this ship design. The firing angles of the port-aft and starboard-aft phaser banks cover farther aft than the lateral mounts on most other vessels. (This is good, since the rear phaser mount has a very narrow field of fire.) The Excelsior, however, has only one forward phaser, which is abnormal for a large ship. This can be a major detriment with a slow recharge rate, and devastating if the enemy is targeting systems with weapons or boarding parties. You need lose only one phaser bank to lose all forward primary weapon coverage.

NEBULA-CLASS "BATTLECRUISER"

Nebula-class starships, compact versions of Galaxy-class vessels, were originally designed for specialized science and exploration missions. Like most Starfleet vessels, these ships were reconfigured for combat-oriented roles after the Borg threat and the ongoing Dominion War stretched the fleet to its limits. Though its armament is as good as that of other battlecruiser-class vessels, the Nebula isn't as fast or maneuverable as its Klingon and Romulan counterparts.

Nebula-Class Battlecruiser (Default Specifications)

Cost in Points	36,839
Total Mass	35,175
Total Impulse Power	737
Total Warp Power Usage	70.67 of 78
Top Speed	20.95
Maneuverability	0.47
Shields	4 F-Shield-VI
Primary Weapons	2 Fore (2 Phaser XS)
	2 Port (1 Phaser XS, 1 empty)
	2 Starboard (1 Phaser XS, 1 empty)
	1 Aft (empty)
	1 360-degree (Phaser XS)
Heavy Weapons	2 Fore (2 Photon Torpedoes)
	2 Aft (1 Photon Torpedo, 1 empty)
Hull Systems	F-Tractor-IV
	F-Armor-III
	F-Transporter-III
Bridge Systems	F-Computer-III
Engines	F-Thruster-IV
	F-Impulse-IV
	F-Warp-VII
Shuttles (Default/Max)	4/8
Marines (Default/Max)	15/30
Mines (Default/Max)	8/32

Nebula-class battlecruiser

When you want to improve your default Nebula-class vessel, consider the following

- Install type-XS phasers in the empty port and starboard mounts.

- Upgrade the 360-degree phaser to type-XF

- Upgrade the thrusters and impulse engines.

Although it's dangerous to approach from the front, a default Nebula-class vessel is virtually defenseless in the rear quarter. This, added to the ship's comparatively slow speed and low maneuverability, make the Nebula vulnerable to enemy vessels from battlecruiser-class on down. Nebula-class ships are definitely alpha-strike vessels. Hit the enemy with all you've got and retreat while re-arming. With a couple of well-planned upgrades, this ship design goes from below average for its class to quite formidable.

GALAXY-CLASS "DREADNOUGHT"

Despite their designation as dreadnoughts, Galaxy-class vessels were originally designed as exploration vessels. Ongoing hostilities have forced many of these starships into combat roles, but their peaceful origins are clearly visible in the Galaxy design. Though you can turn them into formidable warships with some refitting, the heavy battleships fielded by other empires are more than a match for default-configuration Galaxy-class starships.

Galaxy-Class Dreadnought (Default Specifications)

Galaxy-class dreadnought

Cost in Points	40,939
Total Mass	33,275
Total Impulse Power	737
Total Warp Power Usage	74.67 of 78
Top Speed	22.15
Maneuverability	0.50
Shields	4 F-Shield-VII
Primary Weapons	2 Fore (2 Phaser XS)
	2 Port (1 Phaser XS, 1 empty)
	2 Starboard (1 Phaser XS, 1 empty)
	2 Aft (both empty)
	1 360-degree (Phaser XS)
Heavy Weapons	2 Fore (2 Photon Torpedoes)
	2 Aft (1 Photon Torpedo, 1 empty)
Hull Systems	F-Tractor-IV
	F-Armor-III
	F-Transporter-III
Bridge Systems	F-Computer-III
Engines	F-Thruster-IV
	F-Impulse-IV
	F-Warp-VII
Shuttles (Default/Max)	3/6
Marines (Default/Max)	10/20
Mines (Default/Max)	6/24

Of all of the Federation default ship designs, the Galaxy-class arguably has the most unrealized potential. With a little tinkering, this ship of peace converts into a fierce battleship

Add a Phaser-XS to each of the empty port and starboard mounts, and to each of the aft mounts.

- Upgrade the 360-degree phaser to type-XF.

- Add a photon torpedo in the empty aft mount.

- Upgrade the warp drive, thrusters, and impulse engines.

In its default configuration, the Galaxy-class dreadnought performs similarly to the default Nebula-class battlecruiser. Follow the same tactics to achieve success.

SOVEREIGN-CLASS "BATTLESHIP"

The Sovereign-class battleship is the new standard for Federation multi-role starships. Designed for heavy combat, the Sovereign is also well equipped for scientific and exploratory missions. The state-of-the-art weaponry and systems in the default Sovereign configuration put this starship on equal footing with the battleships fielded by the other galactic empires.

Sovereign-Class Battleship (Default Specifications)

Cost in Points	53,139
Total Mass	41,350
Total Impulse Power	878
Total Warp Power Usage	102.6 of 108
Top Speed	21.23
Maneuverability	0.45
Shields	4 F-Shield-VIII
Primary Weapons	2 Fore (2 Phaser XIS)
	1 Port (1 Phaser XIS)
	1 Starboard (1 Phaser XIS)
	4 Aft (all empty)
	1 360-degree (Phaser XIS)
Heavy Weapons	3 Fore (2 Quantum Torpedoes, 1 empty)
	3 Aft (1 Photon Torpedo, 2 empty)
Hull Systems	F-Tractor-V
	F-Armor-IV
	F-Transporter-III
Bridge Systems	F-Computer-III
Engines	F-Thruster-V
	F-Impulse-V
	F-Warp-IX
Shuttles (Default/Max)	3/6
Marines (Default/Max)	10/20
Mines (Default/Max)	6/24

Sovereign-class battleship

You can turn the Sovereign-class battleship into one of the most formidable ships in the game by performing the following upgrades:

- Add a Phaser-XIS to two of the four aft mounts.

- Upgrade the 360-degree phaser to type-XIF.

- Replace the aft photon torpedo with a quantum torpedo.

- Upgrade the warp drive.

As with all large vessels, the Sovereign-class battleship suffers from speed and maneuverability deficits. This is of little consequence against other large vessels, but it's hazardous when you're up against multiple small, fast opponents. As always, keeping your enemies in your forward firing arc is of the utmost importance. In a large, lumbering vessel like this, the addition of aft armament to shake fast ships from your tail takes on even greater importance.

The Klingon Empire

Kahless the Unforgettable, who slew the tyrant Molor and brought order to the Qo'noS, the Klingon homeworld, founded the Klingon Empire more than 1,500 years ago. Formerly allied with the Romulan Star Empire, the Klingons and the Federation were bitter enemies until the destruction of the Klingon moon Praxis threw their Empire into economic turmoil and forced the Klingons to enter peace negotiations with the Federation in 2293. The Klingon Empire and the Federation are now close allies, though some Klingon factions still harbor lingering hostility toward the Federation and long for the old days of glory and battle.

Because the Klingons are a warrior race, their ship designs have always reflected their penchant for battle and conquest. Scientific exploration is secondary to combat in the Klingon Empire.

Unlike the other major empires of the Alpha and Beta Quadrants, a number of extremely old ships still serve in the Klingon fleet. The B'rel Bird of Prey has been in active service for at least 80 years, and K'Tinga-class vessels have changed little from the earliest D-6 and D-7 designs that have served the fleet for well over a century. Even so, Klingon technology has kept up with the times, and their starships sport the latest in weaponry and systems.

The current Imperial Klingon fleet comprises six starship classes. In this chapter, we'll analyze each Klingon vessel available to you and offer recommendations for enhancements and upgrades to improve on the standard designs.

For information on additional Klingon ships and installations, see Appendix A.

BIRD OF PREY (B'REL)-CLASS "FRIGATE"

"It is a good day to die...but the day is not yet over."—Ancient Klingon philosophy

The B'rel-class Bird of Prey is a venerable design that continues to serve widely throughout the Klingon fleet. Though its armament is less potent than that of Federation and Romulan frigates, the Bird of Prey makes up for that deficit in speed and maneuverability.

Bird of Prey (B'rel)-Class Frigate (Default Specifications)

Cost in Points	12,824
Total Mass	9,975
Total Impulse Power	535
Total Warp Power Usage	19.33 of 22
Top Speed	53.63
Maneuverability	1.30
Shields	K-Shield-III (fore)
	K-Shield-II (port and starboard)
	K-Shield-I (aft)
Primary Weapons	2 Fore (2 Disruptor IF)
Heavy Weapons	1 Fore (Photon Torpedo)
Hull Systems	K-Tractor-I
	K-Armor-I
	K-Transporter-I
Bridge Systems	K-Computer-I
	K-Cloak-I
Engines	K-Thruster-I
	K-Impulse-I
	K-Warp-I
Shuttles (Default/Max)	1/2
Marines (Default/Max)	4/8
Mines (Default/Max)	2/8

Bird of Prey (B'rel)-class frigate

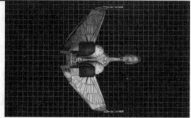

TIP

When commanding a small, vulnerable vessel such as a Bird of Prey, the cloaking device is a vital part of your strategy. Just remember that a few solid hits on your unshielded hull are all it takes to wipe you out, so stay out of your enemy's weapons arc when you engage and disengage your cloak.

With some system upgrades, you can bring the Bird of Prey up to nearly the combat strength of opposing frigates, though you lose some of the vessel's speed and maneuverability in the process. Upgrade recommendations include

- Upgrade both disruptors to type-IIF.

- Upgrade the armor.

Unlike Federation starships, Klingon vessels have aft weapon options as a general rule (although few of their default designs take advantage of them). The Bird of Prey is the only exception to this rule. There is no way to cover aft quarter, so cloak and move out of range between attack runs while you come about. This is greatly facilitated by the B'rel's superior speed and maneuverability. A stock Bird of Prey, properly handled, can inflict serious damage on just about any starship.

K'VORT-CLASS "DESTROYER"

Though visually similar to the B'rel Bird of Prey, the K'Vort-class destroyer is a much larger, better-armed vessel. The K'Vort has primary weapons advantage over both Federation and Romulan destroyers, though the Norway-class has an edge in heavy weapons, especially in its default configuration. The K'Vort is the most maneuverable ship in its class.

K'Vort-Class Destroyer (Default Specifications)

K'Vort-class destroyer

Cost in Points	17,324
Total Mass	13,250
Total Impulse Power	535
Total Warp Power Usage	27.33 of 30
Top Speed	40.38
Maneuverability	0.98
Shields	K-Shield-IV (fore)
	K-Shield-III (port and starboard)
	K-Shield-II (aft)
Primary Weapons	4 Fore (4 Disruptor I)
	1 Aft (empty)
Heavy Weapons	2 Fore (1 Photon Torpedo, 1 empty)
Hull Systems	K-Tractor-II
	K-Armor-I
	K-Transporter-I
Bridge Systems	K-Computer-I
	K-Cloak-I
Engines	K-Thruster-I
	K-Impulse-I
	K-Warp-III
Shuttles (Default/Max)	2/3
Marines (Default/Max)	5/10
Mines (Default/Max)	2/8

Recommended system upgrades include the following:

- Upgrade two of the forward disruptors to type-II.

- Add a Disruptor-II to the aft attachment point.

- Upgrade the armor.

- Upgrade the warp drive.

In its default configuration, the K'Vort suffers the same weakness as the Bird of Prey—no rear weapons coverage. Actually, even if you add a rear weapon, your coverage is still very limited. This ship is designed for frontal assault. Study the weaknesses of your enemy's ship and use your cloak to get within range on the enemy's weakest quarter. Decloak, cut loose with everything you've got, and recloak before your opponent can react.

K'TINGA-CLASS "LIGHT CRUISER"

The tried-and-true K'Tinga-class has served in the Klingon fleet longer than any other design. These ships were once considered heavy cruisers, though by modern standards their classification has been downgraded. Even so, the default loadout of this ship is superior to that of any other ship in its class, and its speed and maneuverability are impressive for a ship of its size.

K'Tinga-Class Light Cruiser (Default Specifications)

Cost in Points	22,584	
Total Mass	16,000	
Total Impulse Power	589	
Total Warp Power Usage	41.33 of 45	
Top Speed	36.81	
Maneuverability	0.94	
Shields	K-Shield-IV (fore)	
	K-Shield-III (port and starboard)	
	K-Shield-II (aft)	
Primary Weapons	2 Fore (2 Disruptor II)	
	1 Port (Disruptor II)	
	1 Starboard (Disruptor II)	
	2 Aft (both empty)	
Heavy Weapons	2 Fore (1 Photon Torpedo, 1 empty)	
	2 Aft (1 Photon Torpedo, 1 empty)	
Hull Systems	K-Tractor-II	
	K-Armor-II	
	K-Transporter-I	
Bridge Systems	K-Computer-I	
	K-Cloak-I	
Engines	K-Thruster-II	
	K-Impulse-II	
	K-Warp-V	
Shuttles (Default/Max)	1/3	
Marines (Default/Max)	6/12	
Mines (Default/Max)	3/12	

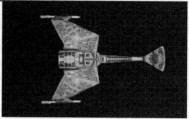

K'Tinga-class light cruiser

The default K'Tinga configuration is actually quite impressive. There isn't a lot of room for upgrades, but there are a few areas where you can improve the ship's performance:

- Upgrade the port, starboard, and rear shields.

- Add a disruptor-II to each of the aft attachment points.

- Move the aft photon torpedo to the empty forward mount.

- Downgrade the impulse engine (to free up some mass) and upgrade the warp drive.

K'Tinga-class ships, true to their origins, fight like heavy cruisers. They are, in fact, an almost even match for both Federation and Romulan heavy cruisers in battle with the right commander. Your forward weaponry is limited, so use your maneuverability to bring your port and starboard disruptors into play in each pass. An excellent K'Tinga tactic is to decloak broadside to your target, unload the facing disruptor, turn toward the target and fire the forward weapons, continue your turn (unloading the opposite lateral disruptor and the aft photon), and then re-engage your cloak as you retreat for the next pass.

FEK'LHR-CLASS "HEAVY CRUISER"

The Fek'lhr-class recently replaced the K'Tinga as the frontline ship of the Klingon battle fleet. As is true with most Klingon starships, this vessel has good speed and maneuverability for its size. In the heavy cruiser class, this is quite pronounced. In fact, this ship handles more like a light cruiser than a heavy one.

Fek'lhr-Class Heavy Cruiser (Default Specifications)

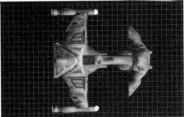

Fek'lhr-class heavy cruiser

Cost in Points	28,559
Total Mass	23,250
Total Impulse Power	589
Total Warp Power Usage	49.00 of 53
Top Speed	25.33
Maneuverability	0.65
Shields	K-Shield-VI (fore and aft)
	K-Shield-V (port and starboard)
	K-Shield-IV (aft)
Primary Weapons	2 Fore (2 Disruptor II)
	1 Port (Disruptor II)
	1 Starboard (Disruptor II)
	2 Aft (both empty)
Heavy Weapons	2 Fore (2 Photon Torpedoes)
	2 Aft (both empty)
Hull Systems	K-Tractor-III
	K-Armor-II
	K-Transporter-II
Bridge Systems	K-Computer-II
	K-Cloak-I
Engines	K-Thruster-II
	K-Impulse-II
	K-Warp-VI
Shuttles (Default/Max)	2/3
Marines (Default/Max)	10/20
Mines (Default/Max)	3/12

Suggested Fek'lhr upgrades include

- Upgrade the port, starboard, and aft shields.

- Add a type-II disruptor in each of the aft mounts.

- Upgrade the warp drive, impulse engines, and thrusters.

The Fek'lhr's weapon configuration is identical to that of the K'Tinga, except that (by default) the second photon torpedo is mounted forward instead of aft. This means that K'Tinga strategies apply to this vessel as well.

Make full use of your maneuverability and speed advantages when up against opponents of the same class to stay out of the enemy's strongest weapon arcs. Between the cloaking device and the Fek'lhr's superior handling characteristics, you can do some serious damage to most opponents that come your way.

VOR'CHA-CLASS "HEAVY BATTLECRUISER"

Klingon battlecruisers, like their heavy cruisers, have amazing speed and maneuverability for their size. Their forward firepower potential surpasses that of Romulan and Federation battlecruisers, though this advantage isn't fully realized in the default design.

Vor'cha-Class Heavy Battlecruiser (Default Specifications)

Cost in Points	33,684
Total Mass	28,625
Total Impulse Power	829
Total Warp Power Usage	52.33 of 66
Top Speed	29.90
Maneuverability	0.68
Shields	K-Shield-VII (fore)
	K-Shield-VI (port and starboard)
	K-Shield-V (aft)
Primary Weapons	4 Fore (2 Disruptor III, 2 empty)
	4 Aft (all empty)
Heavy Weapons	2 Fore (2 Photon Torpedoes)
	1 Aft (empty)
Hull Systems	K-Tractor-IV
	K-Armor-III
	K-Transporter-II
Bridge Systems	K-Computer-II
	K-Cloak-I
Engines	K-Thruster-IV
	K-Impulse-IV
	K-Warp-VII
Shuttles (Default/Max)	2/4
Marines (Default/Max)	10/20
Mines (Default/Max)	4/16

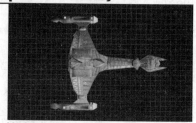

Vor'cha-class heavy battlecruiser

Much of the Vor'cha's massive firepower potential is unrealized in the default configuration, so additional weaponry tops the suggested upgrade list for this vessel:

- Equalize the shields all the way around.

- Add a type-III disruptor to each of the empty forward mounts.

- Add type-II disruptors to all four aft mounts. (If you have to pick and choose your aft weapons, opt for the two outer attachment points. They cover a wider arc than the two center ones.)

- Upgrade your warp drive, impulse engines, and thrusters.

The Vor'cha is vulnerable to lateral and aft attacks in default configuration and, even if you upgrade your weapons to the maximum, the ship still has no coverage directly to port and starboard. You must avoid broadside engagements in this ship. Take advantage of the Vor'cha's maneuverability and speed. It's the only way you can bring your weapons to bear and protect your flanks. Don't lose this advantage by overloading the ship.

NEGH'VAR-CLASS "BATTLESHIP"

The most powerful vessel in the Klingon fleet also enjoys good maneuverability and speed for a ship of its size. The Negh'var's forward firepower surpasses that of the Sovereign-class and equals that of the Warbird-class (though Negh'var is slightly less versatile than the Warbird). In the heavy weapons category, this ship is lacking by comparison to other battleships. Overall, a head-to-head battle between a Negh'var and a Sovereign (default configurations) tends to favor the Negh'var. In a battle with the Romulans, the Warbird's plasma torpedoes give it a distinct advantage.

Negh'var-Class Battleship (Default Specifications)

Cost in Points	50,414
Total Mass	39,800
Total Impulse Power	1,124
Total Warp Power Usage	89.00 of 97
Top Speed	28.24
Maneuverability	0.60
Shields	K-Shield-IX (fore)
	K-Shield-VIII (port and starboard)
	K-Shield-VII (aft)
Primary Weapons	5 Fore (4 Disruptor IV, 1 empty)
	1 Port (empty)
	1 Starboard (empty)
	2 Aft (both empty)
Heavy Weapons	2 Fore (2 Photon Torpedoes)
	2 Aft (1 Photon Torpedo, 1 empty)
Hull Systems	K-Tractor-V
	K-Armor-III
	K-Transporter-III

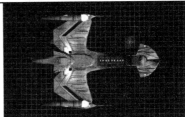

Negh'var-class battleship

Bridge Systems	K-Computer-III
	K-Cloak-I
Engines	K-Thruster-V
	K-Impulse-V
	K-Warp-IX
Shuttles (Default/Max)	3/6
Marines (Default/Max)	10/20
Mines (Default/Max)	6/24

The Negh'var can handle some impressive weaponry, but just about any weapon upgrade overtaxes your warp power, so expect to spend a lot of prestige to get the ship up to its maximum potential:

- Add type-III disruptors to the port and starboard mounts.

- Add type-II disruptors to each of the aft mounts.

- Upgrade your warp drive and impulse engines.

In a ship this big, cloaking is your friend. Use it to stay hidden and out of range until you can lumber around and bring the enemy into your primary weapons arc, then close in for the kill.

The default Negh'var sacrifices lateral and aft weapon coverage in favor of forward firepower. That means that you need to avoid broadside confrontations and keep the enemy off your tail. Though it's quite maneuverable for a ship its size, the Negh'var doesn't have the agility and speed of smaller ships, so be extra cautious not to expose your vulnerable quarters to the enemy. If you get into an unhealthy situation that you can't maneuver out of in real space, use your warp drive to retreat and gain a more favorable position.

6

The Romulan Star Empire

The Romulan Star Empire is one of the most feared and mysterious races in known space. Humans first encountered the Romulans in the mid-22nd century, an encounter that led to a war between Earth and the Romulan Empire in about 2160. After the war, the Romulan Neutral Zone—a demilitarized zone along the border of Romulan space—was established, and it exists to this day.

The Romulans had intermittent contact with the other empires of the Alpha and Beta Quadrants over the centuries, including a short alliance with the Klingon Empire. However, they remained largely reclusive until an incident along the Neutral Zone in 2364—the destruction of several Romulan colonies, apparently perpetrated by the Borg—once again brought the Romulans to the forefront of galactic events. The Romulans have since remained as mysterious as ever, shifting their alliances as they see fit to take advantage of whatever situation arises.

Like Klingon vessels, Romulan ships are designed primarily with combat in mind, though Romulan designs generally depend on the stealth of the cloaking device rather than brute strength. The Romulans operate five basic hull types and variants thereof. Unlike opposing fleets, the Romulan fleet is composed entirely of relatively new starship designs that bear little resemblance to the ships they operated 80 years earlier.

This chapter analyzes the Romulan starships that are available to you in the game and offers design and upgrade suggestions for each. For information on other Romulan ships and Romulan installations, see Appendix A.

TALON-CLASS "FRIGATE"

"We are back."—Commander Tebok

Romulan Talon-class frigates are actually stripped-down destroyers. The design of this vessel is very much in line with that of the Federation Saber-class, though the Talon has a slight edge in handling.

Talon-Class Frigate (Default Specifications)

Cost in Points	14,049
Total Mass	10,150
Total Impulse Power	457
Total Warp Power Usage	25.33 of 27
Top Speed	45.02
Maneuverability	1.13
Shields	4 R-Shield-II
Primary Weapons	3 Fore (3 R-Disruptor I)
Heavy Weapons	1 Fore (Light Plasma Torpedo)
Hull Systems	R-Tractor-I
	R-Armor-I
	R-Transporter-I
Bridge Systems	R-Computer-I
	R-Cloak-I
Engines	R-Thruster-I
	R-Impulse-I
	R-Warp-I
Shuttles (Default/Max)	1/2
Marines (Default/Max)	4/8
Mines (Default/Max)	2/8

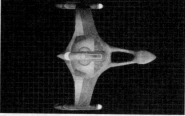

Talon-class frigate

TIP

Fast weapons are undesirable if your strategy involves heavy use of the cloaking device. Only ships that can fire multiple volleys while standing head to head with an enemy take advantage of the full damage potential of fast-charging weapons. Since you usually get only one shot in between decloaking and recloaking, you're better off with weapons that deliver more damage in a single shot than ones that recharge quickly but deliver less damage.

Although the Talon has a very solid default design, you can turn it into an even more formidable ship by making the following upgrades:

- Upgrade the two outer disruptors to type-II.

- Upgrade the warp drive.

Romulan ships are, for the most part, designed to deliver a frontal assault. Typical Romulan battle tactics involve sneaking up on a target while cloaked, cutting loose with an alpha-strike, then recloaking and retreating for another run. The Talon is no exception, and as a result it has no lateral or aft weaponry. This means that keeping your opponent in the forward arc at all times is a must, especially when fighting Klingon ships, which are faster and more maneuverable. Klingon vessels are difficult to shake when they get behind you.

When commanding a small, lightly armored cloaking vessel like a Talon, it's especially important to remember not to cloak or decloak within an enemy's weapons arcs if at all possible. It takes only a couple of unshielded hits to ruin your day.

FALCON-CLASS "DESTROYER"

The Falcon-class destroyer is very similar to the Talon. The biggest difference is the additional forward heavy-weapons mount and the default loadout. The advantage of this design is that it has good maneuverability and speed. The disadvantage is that it has less offensive potential than the destroyers fielded by the Federation and Klingons.

Falcon-Class Destroyer (Default Specifications)

Cost in Points	16,694
Total Mass	13,400
Total Impulse Power	457
Total Warp Power Usage	32.33 of 36
Top Speed	34.10
Maneuverability	0.86
Shields	4 R-Shield-III
Primary Weapons	3 Fore (2 R-Disruptor II, 1 empty)
Heavy Weapons	2 Fore (1 Light Plasma Torpedo, 1 empty)
Hull Systems	R-Tractor-II
	R-Armor-I
	R-Transporter-I
Bridge Systems	R-Computer-I
	R-Cloak-I
Engines	R-Thruster-I
	R-Impulse-I
	R-Warp-III
Shuttles (Default/Max)	2/3
Marines (Default/Max)	5/10
Mines (Default/Max)	2/8

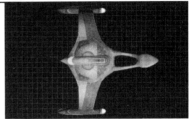

Falcon-class destroyer

With a few changes, you can make a Falcon a good match for any other destroyer design. Suggested changes include

• Add a Disruptor II to the empty attachment point.

• Upgrade the armor. (Because cloaking is a big part of Romulan strategy, extra armor is a must for those vulnerable seconds when you cloak and decloak.)

• Upgrade the warp drive.

Because the design of the Falcon is nearly identical to that of the Talon, all of the same tips and cautions apply.

SHRIKE-CLASS "LIGHT CRUISER"

The Shrike is the smallest Romulan vessel that takes advantage of the superior heavy weaponry available to this race in its default configuration. Medium plasma torpedoes are more powerful than photon torpedoes, and that can be enough to turn the tide of a battle. Even so, default Shrikes still have a heavy weapon deficit (number-wise) versus both Federation light cruisers, and they lack the lateral weapon coverage of the default Klingon K'Tinga design.

Shrike-Class Light Cruiser (Default Specifications)

Cost in Points	20,734
Total Mass	17,600
Total Impulse Power	549
Total Warp Power Usage	39.33 of 43
Top Speed	31.19
Maneuverability	0.76
Shields	4 R-Shield-IV
Primary Weapons	3 Fore (2 R-Disruptor II, 1 empty)
	1 Port (empty)
	1 Starboard (empty)
Heavy Weapons	2 Fore (1 Medium Plasma Torpedo, 1 empty)
Hull Systems	R-Tractor-II
	R-Armor-II
	R-Transporter-II
Bridge Systems	R-Computer-II
	R-Cloak-I
Engines	R-Thruster-II
	R-Impulse-II
	R-Warp-IV
Shuttles (Default/Max)	1/3
Marines (Default/Max)	6/12
Mines (Default/Max)	3/12

Shrike-class light cruiser

Suggested Shrike upgrades include the following:

- Upgrade the forward shield.

- Add a Disruptor-II to the empty forward mount.

- Add a medium plasma torpedo to the empty heavy-weapon mount.

- Upgrade the warp drive.

Like its smaller counterparts, the Shrike is primarily designed as a frontal assault vessel, and as such has minimal lateral-weapons cover and no aft weapons whatsoever. The maneuverability of this light cruiser, however, is sufficient to keep the enemy off your tail if you're careful. As always, make heavy use of the cloaking device. The tactics of every Romulan vessel are built around invisibility. Romulan ships smaller than Hawk class have a tough time winning in a fair fight.

HAWK-CLASS "HEAVY CRUISER"

The Hawk has the potential to out-gun any ship in its class, and even in its default configuration, it can take on any Federation or Klingon default heavy cruiser with little difficulty. Although bested by the Klingon Fek'lhr in performance, the Hawk is still sprightly for its size.

Hawk-Class Heavy Cruiser (Default Specifications)

Cost in Points	27,034
Total Mass	22,475
Total Impulse Power	549
Total Warp Power Usage	53.33 of 61
Top Speed	24.43
Maneuverability	0.59
Shields	4 R-Shield-V
Primary Weapons	3 Fore (2 R-Disruptor II, 1 empty)
	1 Port (empty)
	1 Starboard (empty)
	2 Aft (both empty)
Heavy Weapons	2 Fore (2 Medium Plasma Torpedoes)
	1 Aft (empty)
Hull Systems	R-Tractor-III
	R-Armor-III
	R-Transporter-III
Bridge Systems	R-Computer-III
	R-Cloak-I
Engines	R-Thruster-II
	R-Impulse-II
	R-Warp-VI
Shuttles (Default/Max)	2/3
Marines (Default/Max)	6/12
Mines (Default/Max)	3/12

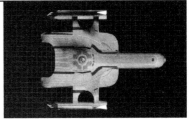

Hawk-class heavy cruiser

It only takes a couple of strategic enhancements to turn the Hawk into the finest heavy cruiser available:

- Add a Disruptor-II to the empty forward mount.

- Add a Disruptor-II to the port and starboard mounts.

- Upgrade the warp drive, impulse engines, and thrusters.

NOTE

Alternatively, when upgrading the Hawk, consider forgoing lateral weapons for a pair of Disruptor-IIs and a medium plasma torpedo in the aft mounts. This gives you a respectable aft attack in addition to your killer frontal attack.

With the default Hawk, as with all Romulan ships, remember that the alpha-strike is your key to success. Make sure all of your forward weapons are bearing on your target when you decloak for your strike so that you can deliver as much damage as possible in a single volley.

RAPTOR-CLASS "HEAVY BATTLECRUISER"

Above heavy-cruiser class, Romulan ships are downright nasty. In the battlecruiser category, the default Raptor is more than a match for its Klingon and Federation counterparts. No ship this size can match the awesome destructive potential of three medium plasma torpedoes in a single firing arc, even with extensive upgrades.

Raptor-Class Heavy Battlecruiser (Default Specifications)

Cost in Points	36,894
Total Mass	27,950
Total Impulse Power	793
Total Warp Power Usage	72.00 of 78
Top Speed	28.37
Maneuverability	0.61
Shields	4 R-Shield-VI
Primary Weapons	4 Fore (2 R-Disruptor III, 2 empty)
	2 Aft (both empty)
Heavy Weapons	3 Fore (3 Medium Plasma Torpedoes)
	1 Aft (empty)
Hull Systems	R-Tractor-IV
	R-Armor-III
	R-Transporter-IV
Bridge Systems	R-Computer-V
	R-Cloak-I
Engines	R-Thruster-IV
	R-Impulse-IV
	R-Warp-VII
Shuttles (Default/Max)	2/4
Marines (Default/Max)	10/20
Mines (Default/Max)	4/16

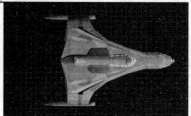

Raptor-class heavy battlecruiser

Believe it or not, there are actually some improvements you can make to this ship class:

- Add a Disruptor-III to each of the empty forward mounts.

- Upgrade one of the existing plasma torpedoes from medium to heavy.

- Upgrade the armor.

- Upgrade the warp drive.

You have little to fear when you're commanding a Raptor against default-configuration enemies in the same size class and, if you make a few upgrades, ships your size and smaller will run in fear.

WARBIRD (D'DERIDEX)-CLASS "BATTLESHIP"

The Romulan Warbird is the largest non-Borg ship in the game. Despite this, it can out-maneuver a Federation Sovereign-class battleship, which is about half the Warbird's size. No ship in this class can match the Warbird's overall combined firepower (though the Negh'var comes close).

Warbird (D'Deridex)-Class Battleship (Default Specifications)

Cost in Points	50,734
Total Mass	37,750
Total Impulse Power	947
Total Warp Power Usage	116.0 of 123
Top Speed	25.09
Maneuverability	0.50
Shields	4 R-Shield-VIII
Primary Weapons	4 Fore (4 R-Disruptor IV)
	2 Aft (both empty)
	1 360-degree (empty)
Heavy Weapons	3 Fore (2 Medium Plasma Torpedoes,
	1 Heavy Plasma Torpedo)
Hull Systems	R-Tractor-V
	R-Armor-IV
	R-Transporter-V
Bridge Systems	R-Computer-V
	R-Cloak-I
Engines	R-Thruster-V
	R-Impulse-V
	R-Warp-IX
Shuttles (Default/Max)	3/6
Marines (Default/Max)	10/20
Mines (Default/Max)	6/24

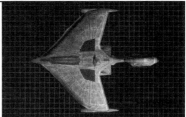

Warbird (D'Deridex)-class
battleship

Suggested Warbird refits and additions include

• Add a Disruptor IVF to the 360-degree mount. (Using a fast disruptor on this mount allows you to fire it a second time in your side or aft arc as you turn away after your frontal strike.)

• Upgrade the armor.

• Upgrade the impulse engines and thrusters.

The biggest drawback of the Warbird is that, despite the fact that it's reasonably maneuverable for its size, it's difficult to play the usual "submarine warfare" game that you play with other Romulan ships, especially if you're up against a smaller, more maneuverable enemy. Targets won't sit still while you swing around to bring your forward weapons to bear. For this reason, you might find yourself fighting out in the open more often in a Warbird. This ship can withstand a great deal of damage, but if you can't bring your weapons to bear in a reasonable amount of time, use your warp drive and cloaking device to get some distance, and come around for another pass. In its default configuration, a Warbird has no weapon coverage whatsoever beyond the forward arc, so it's susceptible to enemies that sneak up from behind.

7

The Borg Collective

Originating in the Delta Quadrant, the cybernetic race known as the Borg operate as a collective—a hive mind in which individuality is erased and each being becomes merely a drone, a working part of the collective whole. The Borg gain technology through the assimilation of other species, and are responsible for the extinction or near-extinction of hundreds, perhaps thousands, of races throughout the galaxy. Because of their vast technological knowledge, the Borg are able to adapt to nearly any offensive, defensive, or tactical systems they encounter.

The first confirmed human contact with the Borg occurred in 2365, when an entity from the Q continuum propelled the *USS Enterprise* into Borg space. Since then, the Borg have launched two invasions into Federation space, resulting in thousands of casualties and the loss of more than 40 Federation starships.

The Borg fleet consists of only a handful of starship designs and variations thereof, seven of which are available to you in the game. For information on additional Borg ships and installations, see Appendix A.

PYRAMID

"Resistance is futile."—The Borg

The Pyramid is the smallest Borg starship in the game. In default configuration, Pyramids are in line performance- and weapons-wise with the frigates employed by other empires. With some modification, this ship easily outguns others of similar size.

TIP

A major problem with Borg ships is that it's hard to tell which way they're facing. When you're controlling a Borg ship, use the passive sensors to determine your facing in relation to your target's position. (Forward is always up on the passive sensor display.) When you're fighting the Borg, watch the shield-facing indicator on the target data display to know which side of the Borg ship you're looking at.

Pyramid (Default Specifications)

Cost in Points	12,459
Total Mass	8,750
Total Impulse Power	429
Total Warp Power Usage	17.00 of 26
Top Speed	49.03
Maneuverability	1.14
Shields	N/A
Primary Weapons	1 Fore (Light Cutting Beam)
	1 Port (empty)
	1 Starboard (Light Cutting Beam)
	1 Aft (Light Cutting Beam)
	1 360-degree (empty)
Heavy Weapons	1 Fore (Gravimetric Torpedo)
	1 Aft (empty)
Hull Systems	B-Tractor-I
	B-Armor-I
	B-Transporter-I
Bridge Systems	B-Computer-I
Engines	B-Thruster-I
	B-Impulse-I
	B-Warp-II
Shuttles (Default/Max)	1/2
Marines (Default/Max)	6/12
Mines (Default/Max)	2/8

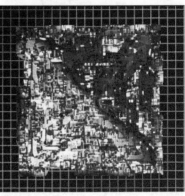

A Borg Pyramid (the Collective's equivalent to a frigate)

Because of mass limitations, it's difficult to max out a Pyramid's weapon potential. You can, however, improve the ship's offensive performance with the following refits:

- Upgrade the forward cutting beam from light to medium.

- Remove nonforward cutting beams (to free up some mass) and install a medium cutting beam-F in the 360-degree mount.

- Upgrade the armor.

The one advantage enjoyed by Pyramids over other frigates is heavy weapon range. Gravimetric torpedoes have a slight range advantage over photon and light plasma torpedoes.

PYRAMID PRIME

The Pyramid Prime is a heavier variant of the basic Pyramid design that serves as the Borg equivalent of the destroyers fielded by other empires. Almost identical to the Pyramid, the only real differences between the ships is the additional mass tolerance of the Prime model, which allows for more extensive modifications but also detracts slightly from the ship's speed and performance.

Pyramid Prime (Default Specifications)

Cost in Points	13,359
Total Mass	11,050
Total Impulse Power	429
Total Warp Power Usage	17.00 of 26
Top Speed	38.82
Maneuverability	0.90
Shields	N/A
Primary Weapons	1 Fore (Light Cutting Beam)
	1 Port (empty)
	1 Starboard (Light Cutting Beam)
	1 Aft (Light Cutting Beam)
	1 360-degree (empty)
Heavy Weapons	1 Fore (Gravimetric Torpedo)
	1 Aft (empty)
Hull Systems	B-Tractor-I
	B-Armor-I
	B-Transporter-I
Bridge Systems	B-Computer-I
Engines	B-Thruster-I
	B-Impulse-I
	B-Warp-II
Shuttles (Default/Max)	1/2
Marines (Default/Max)	8/16
Mines (Default/Max)	2/8

More extensive refits are possible on the Pyramid Prime, making it much more deadly than the basic Pyramid. Suggestions include

- Upgrade the forward cutting beam from light to medium.

- Add a medium-F cutting beam to the 360-degree mount.

- Upgrade the armor.

- Upgrade the warp drive.

Because the basic configuration of this ship and the basic Pyramid are the same, the same tactics apply to both, although you have to compensate slightly for the reduced speed and performance of the Prime model.

DIAMOND

Diamonds perform similarly to the light cruisers fielded by the other empires, and their default weapon loadout is also similar, however, the configuration of this ship's weapon mounts gives it firepower versatility that other ships in this class are hard-pressed to match.

Diamond (Default Specifications)

Cost in Points	24,084
Total Mass	17,550
Total Impulse Power	481
Total Warp Power Usage	44.00 of 50
Top Speed	27.41
Maneuverability	0.74
Shields	N/A
Primary Weapons	1 Fore (Light Cutting Beam)
	1 Port (Light Cutting Beam)
	1 Starboard (Light Cutting Beam)
	1 Aft (empty)
	2 360-degree (1 Light Cutting Beam, 1 empty)
Heavy Weapons	1 Fore (Gravimetric Torpedo)
	1 Port (Gravimetric Torpedo)
	1 Starboard (Gravimetric Torpedo)
	1 Aft (Gravimetric Torpedo)
Hull Systems	B-Tractor-II
	B-Armor-II
	B-Transporter-II
Bridge Systems	B-Computer-II
Engines	B-Thruster-III
	B-Impulse-II
	B-Warp-V
Shuttles (Default/Max)	1/3
Marines (Default/Max)	12/24
Mines (Default/Max)	3/12

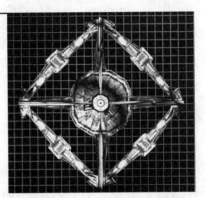

The Borg Diamond (the Collective's equivalent to a light cruiser)

When you're upgrading a Diamond, primary weapons are the focus. Few other ships in the game have two 360-degree weapon mounts, and you should make use of both of them! Refit possibilities include the following:

- Remove the port and starboard cutting beams and the aft gravimetric torpedo (to free up mass).

- Add a medium cutting beam-F to the empty 360-degree mount and upgrade the existing 360-degree cutting beam to the same.

- Upgrade your impulse engines and thrusters.

Chapter 7: The Borg Collective

The number one problem with a default Diamond is primary weapon range compared with other default ships in its class. Light cutting beams have shorter range than the type-II disruptors and type-X phasers typically found on other light cruisers. A good Borg light vessel tactic is to use your extended heavy weapon range to weaken the enemy shields, then warp in for a full-on cutting-beam barrage. After you empty your weapon banks, warp back out of range until your weapons cycle.

DIAMOND PRIME

The Diamond Prime is a heavier version of the basic Diamond that is designed to combat heavy cruiser-class vessels. Like the Pyramid Prime, the difference between this ship and its non-Prime counterpart is added mass for upgrades. Because of the slight variance in default loadout, the Diamond Prime's performance characteristics are very similar to those of the basic Diamond.

Diamond Prime (Default Specifications)

Cost in Points	27,784
Total Mass	19,550
Total Impulse Power	558
Total Warp Power Usage	47.00 of 60
Top Speed	28.54
Maneuverability	0.66
Shields	N/A
Primary Weapons	1 Fore (Light Cutting Beam)
	1 Port (Light Cutting Beam)
	1 Starboard (Light Cutting Beam)
	1 Aft (Light Cutting Beam)
	2 360-degree (1 Light Cutting Beam, 1 empty)
Heavy Weapons	1 Fore (Gravimetric Torpedo)
	1 Port (Gravimetric Torpedo)
	1 Starboard (Gravimetric Torpedo)
	1 Aft (Gravimetric Torpedo)
Hull Systems	B-Tractor-II
	B-Armor-II
	B-Transporter-II
Bridge Systems	B-Computer-II
Engines	B-Thruster-III
	B-Impulse-III
	B-Warp-VI
Shuttles (Default/Max)	1/3
Marines (Default/Max)	14/28
Mines (Default/Max)	3/12

As with the basic Diamond, you should take advantage of the twin 360-degree mounts on this ship when upgrading. Suggestions include

• Remove the port, starboard, and aft cutting beams (to free up mass).

• Add a medium cutting beam-F to the empty 360-degree mount and upgrade the existing 360-degree cutting beam to the same.

- Upgrade the forward cutting beam to medium-F.

- Upgrade your impulse engines and thrusters.

When commanding a Diamond Prime, follow the same combat strategies as you would when commanding a basic Diamond. The performance of this ship should give you an edge over the other empires' heavy cruisers.

SPHERE

When they wish to escalate a conflict, they don't fool around. When a Borg Sphere enters the picture, the other empires can best face the threat by deploying battlecruiser-class vessels. Even then, the Sphere's heavy armor and huge compliment of weapons is a formidable challenge for any default-configuration battlecruiser.

Sphere (Default Specifications)

Cost in Points	36,634
Total Mass	23,975
Total Impulse Power	558
Total Warp Power Usage	70.00 of 73
Top Speed	23.27
Maneuverability	0.54
Shields	N/A
Primary Weapons	2 Fore (1 Medium Cutting Beam, 1 empty)
	2 Port (2 Medium Cutting Beams)
	2 Starboard (2 Medium Cutting Beams)
	1 Aft (empty)
	2 360-degree (both empty)
Heavy Weapons	2 Fore (2 Gravimetric Torpedoes)
	1 Port (Gravimetric Torpedo)
	1 Starboard (Gravimetric Torpedo)
	2 Aft (1 Gravimetric Torpedo, 1 empty)
Hull Systems	B-Tractor-IV
	B-Armor-IV
	B-Transporter-I
Bridge Systems	B-Computer-IV
Engines	B-Thruster-III
	B-Impulse-III
	B-Warp-VII
Shuttles (Default/Max)	2/4
Marines (Default/Max)	18/36
Mines (Default/Max)	4/16

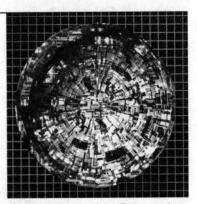

The Borg Sphere (the Collective's equivalent to a heavy battlecruiser)

Despite the fact that this is a formidable vessel in its default state, there are a number of modifications that make a Sphere even deadlier:

- Remove one cutting beam each from port and starboard (your choice). You need to shed some mass so you can...

- Add a medium cutting beam-F to each of the 360-degree mounts.

Firepower versatility is the name of the game with Borg ships, and the Sphere is a great example of this. In default configuration, you can treat it just like most other battlecruiser-class ships: favor the forward arc and stay away from broadside encounters; however, by shifting a couple of your cutting beams to the 360-degree mounts, you can create a ship that is quite deadly from all sides. Refits are highly recommended for Borg ships.

SPHERE PRIME

With additional mass for weapon and other system upgrades, the Sphere Prime turns the basic Sphere design into a ship that is a match for the battleships fielded by other empires—and this isn't even the Borg's most formidable ship! The Sphere Prime is a vessel to be feared.

Sphere Prime (Default Specifications)

Cost in Points	42,399
Total Mass	26,600
Total Impulse Power	670
Total Warp Power Usage	84.00 of 87
Top Speed	25.19
Maneuverability	0.55
Shields	N/A
Primary Weapons	2 Fore (1 Medium Cutting Beam, 1 empty)
	2 Port (2 Medium Cutting Beams)
	2 Starboard (2 Medium Cutting Beams)
	1 Aft (Medium Cutting Beam)
	2 360-degree (both empty)
Heavy Weapons	2 Fore (2 Gravimetric Torpedoes)
	1 Port (Gravimetric Torpedo)
	1 Starboard (Gravimetric Torpedo)
	2 Aft (2 Gravimetric Torpedoe)
Hull Systems	B-Tractor-IV
	B-Armor-IV
	B-Transporter-I
Bridge Systems	B-Computer-IV
Engines	B-Thruster-IV
	B-Impulse-IV
	B-Warp-VIII
Shuttles (Default/Max)	2/4
Marines (Default/Max)	20/40
Mines (Default/Max)	4/16

The suggested upgrades to the Sphere Prime run along similar lines to the Sphere upgrades:

- Free up some mass by replacing one port and one starboard medium cutting beam with light cutting beams.

- Add a medium cutting beam-F to each of the 360-degree mounts.

- Upgrade the transporter.

- Upgrade the warp drive, impulse engines, and thrusters.

    The Sphere Prime is one of the best battleships available, especially when you consider the potential for marine activity. You can take out quite a few enemy systems with as many drones as this ship carries. Take advantage of this by upgrading your transporter to the best model you can afford.

CUBE

The Borg Cube is nothing short of a mobile starbase. In its default configuration, its firepower potential far exceeds that of even a heavily modified Federation, Klingon, or Romulan battleship. When you see a Borg Cube coming your way, be afraid. Be *very* afraid.

Cube (Default Specifications)

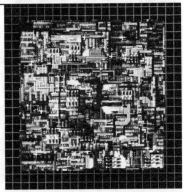

Cost in Points	165,603
Total Mass	46,125
Total Impulse Power	838
Total Warp Power Usage	202.00 of 308
Top Speed	18.17
Maneuverability	0.35
Shields	N/A
Primary Weapons	3 Fore (3 Heavy Cutting Beams)
	1 Port (1 Heavy Cutting Beam)
	1 Starboard (1 Heavy Cutting Beam)
	3 Aft (3 Heavy Cutting Beams)
	2 360-degree (2 Heavy Cutting Beams)
Heavy Weapons	2 Fore (2 Gravimetric Torpedoes)
	2 Port (2 Gravimetric Torpedoes)
	2 Starboards (2 Gravimetric Torpedoes)
	2 Aft (2 Gravimetric Torpedoes)
	2 360-degree (1 Tachyon Pulse, 1 Sheild Inverse Beam)
Hull Systems	B-Tractor-V
	B-Armor-V
	B-Transporter-V
Bridge Systems	B-Computer-V
Engines	B-Thruster-V
	B-Impulse-V
	B-Warp-SB
Shuttles (Default/Max)	3/6
Marines (Default/Max)	40/80
Mines (Default/Max)	6/24

The Borg Cube—the ultimate fighting machine

The Borg always seek perfection, and the Cube is the ultimate example of this. It is devastation incarnate in its default form. There's no need whatsoever to make any upgrades or changes.

The primary disadvantage of the ultra-massive Cube is maneuverability. You can theoretically cut smaller ships to pieces—but, unless they're dumb enough to stay in your most powerful weapon arcs, they can tear you up a little at a time. It's very frustrating.

To counter this effect, take a lesson from the Borg tactics you've seen on television: grab your target with a tractor beam before you open fire. If you tractor the target, you can rotate the enemy around your ship, exposing the victim to every weapons mount you've got. While many players never bother with tractor tactics in combat, as a Borg player, always take advantage of your strong tractor beams to keep faster, more maneuverable enemies at bay.

NOTE

The size and shape of the Borg ships make playing in the default View Screen mode difficult when you are the Borg—your ship tends to eclipse your target most of the time. This is especially true of the Cube. The best viewpoint for close-quarters engagements when playing the Borg is Top-Down (F1) mode.

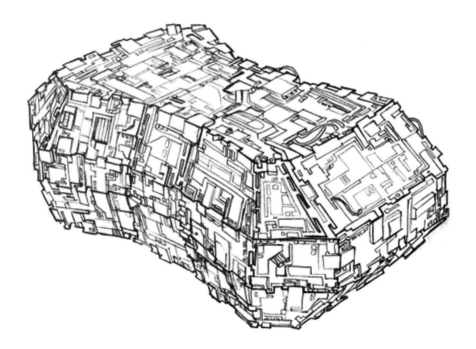

8

Space Dock—
Starship Design

One of the biggest challenges that *SFC* commanders face is learning the strengths and limitations of their vessels and those of their opponents. If your enemy knows more about your ship than you do, you are in for the pounding of a lifetime, but if you understand what your ship is capable of and exploit the weaknesses of your enemy, you can prevail every time.

In *Starfleet Command III*, you can go one step further and actually change the operational parameters of your ship so that the enemy never knows what to expect. Now, you can sit down at the drafting table at Utopia Planetia and take on the role of starship designer. With the ability to customize weapon load out, shield strength, power distribution, and control systems, you can turn standard starship designs into superior vessels that pack a surprise punch for your unsuspecting opponents.

DESIGN BASICS

"If we don't get more power to the warp drive, we're all going to have to get out and push!"—Tom Paris

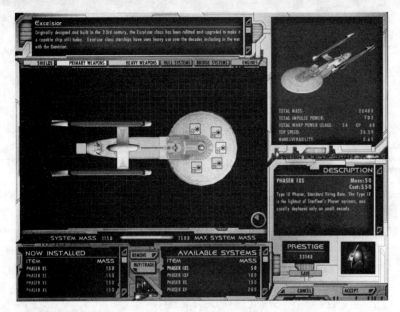

Figure 8.1 In space dock—preparing to refit a starship

Before you start building the ultimate starship (see Figure 8.1), there are some basic design principles you need to understand.

Your ship's overall performance is displayed at all times in the upper-right section of the screen (see Figure 8.2). This display constantly monitors the projected operating parameters of the ship, updating the statistics automatically as you alter the design.

The performance display provides the following information:

Total Mass: This is the mass of the starship's hull plus all of its systems. The more mass you add to a ship, the slower it accelerates and the less maneuverable it becomes.

Total Impulse Power: Impulse engines provide your sublight movement power—your primary motive force during combat. More advanced impulse engines provide more impulse power. High impulse power generally means more speed in combat.

Total Warp Power Usage: All of your ship's non-engine systems draw most of their power from the warp drive. Total warp power usage is the ratio of how much power your ship's systems draw to the total power output of the warp drive.

WARNING

When the left-hand number in your total warp power usage ratio is higher than the one on the right, your ship's systems require more power than the warp drive is able to provide. In battle, this means that you cannot use all of your systems simultaneously. For example, if you are traveling at high speeds, your weapons recharge slowly (or not at all), shield reinforcement might not be available, and so on. It is always better to have an even ratio of usage to available power if possible.

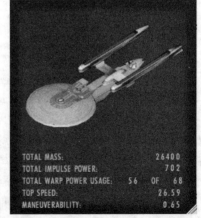

Figure 8.2 The master performance display

Top Speed: This is your top sub-light (combat) speed. Top speed is affected by several factors, including the type of impulse engine and the ship's total mass.

Maneuverability: This stat represents your ship's agility in combat—its turning rate and so on. Thruster type is the primary determiner of maneuverability (better thrusters equal better maneuverability), however, maneuverability decreases as total mass increases.

Performance in the field is the ultimate test of whether a starship design is actually effective, but you can tell a lot about basic handling and power usage before you leave space dock just by checking the master performance display. Starships tend to perform best if they have the following basic performance characteristics:

A total warp power usage ratio equivalent to 1:1 or better. In other words, usage should be equal to or less than the total warp power output.

A top speed of 20 or higher. Slower ships are easy targets. Even a large, well-shielded vessel eventually falls prey to hit-and-run attacks by small, fast-moving ships.

A maneuverability rating of 0.5 or higher. A full complement of quantum torpedoes is useless if you can't bring them to bear. Ships with low maneuverability are usually vaporized before they can get off more than a few shots.

The best way to achieve this kind of performance is to be realistic with your modifications. Base your weapon and system choices on the hull class you select. If your warp power usage is off the scale and your top speed and maneuverability are abysmal, chances are that you're overloading your hull. Face it: that Federation Saber wasn't designed to sport XIIF phasers. A realistic design approach leads to functional starships.

Perhaps the best general advice for improving on the stock starship designs in the game is to add aft-firing weapons. Most of the ships are completely vulnerable from behind. Adding some aft weaponry—even low-power primaries, such as Phaser-IX or Disruptor-I—allows you to get in a close-range parting shot while you swing around for your next attack run.

Finally, there's the issue of cost. Every ship refit costs you some prestige. This is the single most important guiding factor in ship customization in the single-player campaign and in Dynaverse multiplayer games, where prestige is a hard-earned commodity. In skirmish games, where you (or the game host in multiplayer skirmishes) set the prestige point limit, it's less of an issue. A truly good starship designer, however, can create effective custom ships within a set budget. (See "Ships on a Budget" later in this chapter for some examples.)

CUSTOMIZABLE SYSTEMS

Most starship hulls have six customizable system categories (the Borg, who don't use shields, have only five):

- Shields
- Primary weapons
- Heavy weapons
- Hull systems
- Bridge systems
- Engines

Every category has a number of attachment points, each of which can house a single system in that category. The number of attachment points varies depending on hull type. Generally speaking, the bigger the ship, the more attachment points it has in each category.

Every ship system has mass. Regardless of the number of attachment points available, every hull type has a mass limitation associated with each category. Shields and engines are treated as independent mass categories. Primary and heavy weapons share one combined system mass limit, as do hull and bridge systems.

NOTE

Every ship system also has a price (in prestige points) associated with it. In skirmish games, you (or the game's host) can set the number of prestige points at your disposal for ship selection, supply, and refit. In the single-player campaign and the Dynaverse multiplayer game, you must earn prestige points as you go—which means that there are systems that you cannot add to your ship, even if they fit mass-wise, if you haven't earned enough prestige to afford them.

The amount of mass available for each system varies with hull class. Tables 8.1–4 show the maximum mass for every customizable system group for the starships of each empire.

Hull Class	Shields	Weapons (Primary + Secondary)	Ship Systems (Hull Systems + Bridge Systems)	Engines
Saber	6,000	650	1,800	1,850
Norway	8,500	1,000	2,300	2,550
Defiant	10,000	1,150	3,400	4,750
Intrepid	12,000	1,300	3,100	4,500
Akira	20,000	1,600	3,700	6,250
Excelsior	18,000	1,500	5,000	5,400
Nebula	22,000	1,800	5,700	7,800
Galaxy	28,000	2,200	6,500	8,500
Sovereign	32,000	2,900	6,700	9,500

Table 8.1 Federation Starship Max System Mass by Hull Class

Hull Class	Shields	Weapons (Primary + Secondary)	Ship Systems (Hull Systems + Bridge Systems)	Engines
Bird of Prey	6,000	650	1,650	1,800
K'Vort	8,500	1,000	2,300	2,425
K'Tinga	13,000	1,300	3,100	3,500
Fek'lhr	19,000	1,550	3,550	5,200
Vor'cha	26,000	2,100	6,000	7,550
Negh'var	32,000	2,900	6,700	9,000

Table 8.2 Klingon Starship Max System Mass by Hull Class

Hull Class	Shields	Weapons (Primary + Secondary)	Ship Systems (Hull Systems + Bridge Systems)	Engines
Talon	6,000	650	1,650	2,000
Falcon	8,000	1,000	2,300	2,775
Shrike	11,000	1,300	3,100	3,925
Hawk	15,000	1,500	3,550	5,950
Raptor	20,500	2,100	6,000	8,900
Warbird	26,000	2,900	6,700	9,750

Table 8.3 Romulan Starship Max System Mass by Hull Class

Hull Class	Shields	Weapons (Primary + Secondary)	Ship Systems (Hull Systems + Bridge Systems)	Engines
Pyramid	N/A	750	2,300	2,300
Pyramid Prime	N/A	1,150	3,100	3,200
Diamond	N/A	1,450	3,700	4,800
Diamond Prime	N/A	1,700	5,500	6,600
Sphere	N/A	2,350	6,500	8,600
Sphere Prime	N/A	3,200	7,300	10,000
Cube	N/A	6,500	7,300	13,000

Table 8.4 Borg Starship Max System Mass by Hull Class

In the following sections, we'll look at the specifics of each system category, including the limitations of all hull types and the mass requirements of the various weapons and systems.

Shields

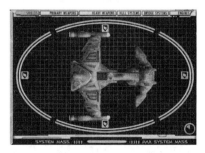

Shield generator attachment

Every starship (with the exception of Borg vessels) has four attachment points for shield generators: forward, aft, port, and starboard. Each shield generator powers the shield corresponding to its hull location.

Table 8.5a and 8.5b list the mass and prestige cost of all shield types.

Most hull classes won't accommodate a full compliment of type-X shields, however, nothing prevents you from mixing and matching shield generator types. Most hull classes have the bulk of their weaponry mounted in forward-firing configurations. That means that your front shield must face your target whenever you fire. If you can't afford the mass or prestige to upgrade all of your shield generators, consider upgrading the forward generator to the highest shield type you can afford. This provides you with an extra measure of protection where you need it most.

NOTE

Borg vessels do not use deflector shields.

| | SHIELD-I | | SHIELD-II | | SHIELD-III | | SHIELD-IV | | SHIELD-V | |
	Mass	Cost	Mass	Cost	Mass	Cost	Mass	Cost	Mass	Cost
Federation	1,000	500	1,500	750	2,000	1,125	2,750	1,500	3,500	2,000
Klingon	1,000	500	1,500	750	2,000	1,125	2,750	1,500	3,500	2,000
Romulan	1,000	500	1,500	750	2,000	1,000	2,500	1,250	3,000	1,500

Table 8.5a Shield Generators I–V Mass and Cost

| | SHIELD-VI | | SHIELD-VII | | SHIELD-VIII | | SHIELD-IX | | SHIELD-X | |
	Mass	Cost	Mass	Cost	Mass	Cost	Mass	Cost	Mass	Cost
Federation	4,250	2,500	5,000	3,250	6,000	4,000	7,000	5,000	8,000	6,000
Klingon	4,250	2,500	5,000	3,250	6,000	4,000	7,000	5,000	8,000	6,000
Romulan	3,500	1,750	4,000	2,000	4,750	2,250	5,500	2,500	6,500	2,750

Table 8.5b Shield Generators VI–X Mass and Cost

WARNING

Shields are not required equipment on any vessel, but this is not the system you want to drop to reduce mass and increase your ship's performance. Don't believe it? Try doing battle in an unshielded ship.

Primary Weapons

Primary weapons—phasers, disruptors, and cutting beams—are the most important offensive systems on your ship. The raw power of heavy weapons is enticing, but don't be tempted to overload your ship with torpedoes and the like at the expense of your primaries. The slow recharge rate of most heavy weapons leaves you vulnerable between attack runs and gives your opponent's shields time to regenerate. You need an array of primary weapons to press your attack. Tables 8.6–8.9 show the mass and cost of all primary weapons.

Weapon	Mass	Prestige Cost
Phaser IXS	50	550
Phaser IXF	100	700
Phaser XS	150	900
Phaser XF	200	1,250
Phaser XIS	250	1,300
Phaser XIF	300	1,600
Phaser XIIS	350	1,650
Phaser XIIF	400	1,900
Pulse Phaser	275	1,250

Table 8.6 Federation Primary Weapons Mass and Cost

Primary weapon attachment points (typical)

Weapon	Mass	Prestige Cost
Disruptor I	50	650
Disruptor IF	100	825
Disruptor II	150	925
Disruptor IIF	200	1,300
Disruptor III	250	1,350
Disruptor IIIF	300	1,600
Disruptor IV	350	1,650
Disruptor IVF	400	1,900

Table 8.7 Klingon Primary Weapons Mass and Cost

Weapon	Mass	Prestige Cost
R-Disruptor I	50	700
R-Disruptor IF	100	850
R-Disruptor II	150	1,025
R-Disruptor IIF	200	1,175
R-Disruptor III	250	1,300
R-Disruptor IIIF	300	1,450
R-Disruptor IV	350	1,600
R-Disruptor IVF	400	1,850

Table 8.8 Romulan Primary Weapons Mass and Cost

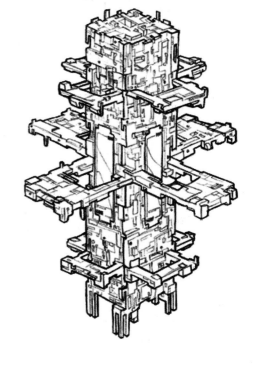

Weapon	Mass	Prestige Cost
Light Cutting Beam	150	725
Light Cutting Beam-F	200	975
Medium Cutting Beam	250	1,075
Medium Cutting Beam-F	300	1,300
Heavy Cutting Beam	350	1,600
Heavy Cutting Beam-F	400	2,400

Table 8.9 Borg Primary Weapons Mass and Cost

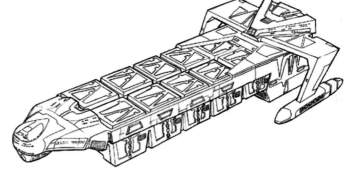

Heavy Weapons

Heavy weapons are the "glamorous" offensive systems. They pack far more per-shot punch than their primary counterparts and are, therefore, much more tempting. The importance of these weapons, however, pales in comparison to primary weapons. They tend to be less accurate, they have slow recharge rates, and they require a lot of power.

While it is usually good to have at least one heavy weapon, it is quite feasible to operate a vessel with no heavy weapons whatsoever. The reverse, however, is not true.

Tables 8.10–8.13 show the mass and cost of all heavy weapons.

Weapon	Mass	Prestige Cost
Photon Torpedo	200	1,000
Quantum Torpedo	300	1,500
Tachyon Pulse	250	2,450
Antimatter Minelayer	200	1,500

Table 8.10 Federation Heavy Weapons Mass and Cost

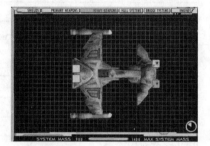

Heavy weapon attachment points (typical)

Weapon	Mass	Prestige Cost
K-Photon Torpedo	200	900
Polaron Torpedo	300	2,200
Tachyon Pulse	250	2,450
Ion Cannon	250	1,350
Antimatter Minelayer	200	1,500

Table 8.11 Klingon Heavy Weapons Mass and Cost

Weapon	Mass	Prestige Cost
Light Plasma Torpedo	200	800
Medium Plasma Torpedo	300	1,200
Heavy Plasma Torpedo	400	1,600
Myotronic Beam	200	2,150
Tachyon Pulse	250	2,450
Antimatter Minelayer	200	1,500

Table 8.12 Romulan Heavy Weapons Mass and Cost

Weapon	Mass	Prestige Cost
Gravametric Torpedo	200	1,300
Shield Inversion Beam	250	1,800
Tachyon Pulse	250	2,450
Antimatter Minelayer	200	1,500

Table 8.13 Borg Heavy Weapons Mass and Cost

Chapter 8: Space Dock—Starship Design

Hull Systems

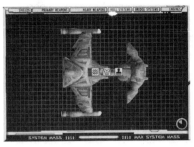

Hull system attachment points
(typical)

Whereas shields and weapons are vital to a successful star-ship design, hull systems—armor, transporters, and tractor beams—are not. If you have to shed some mass to improve performance, this is the best category in which to make your cuts.

Armor

Of the three systems, armor is the most vital. You should always consider at least minimal armor in any ship design. That said, when given the choice between armor and better shields, shields should win every time. If you keep your shields between you and your opponent, you don't need armor.

Table 8.14 lists the mass and cost of all armor types.

	ARMOR-I Mass	Cost	ARMOR-II Mass	Cost	ARMOR-III Mass	Cost	ARMOR-IV Mass	Cost	ARMOR-V Mass	Cost
Federation	1,000	500	1,500	750	2,000	1,125	2,500	1,750	3,000	2,500
Klingon	800	500	1,200	750	1,600	1,125	2,000	1,750	2,400	2,500
Romulan	900	500	1,350	750	1,800	1,125	2,250	1,750	2,700	2,500
Borg	1,000	500	1,500	750	2,000	1,125	2,500	1,750	3,000	2,500

Table 8.14 Armor Systems Mass and Cost

Transporters and Tractor Beams

Transporters and tractor beams are very specialized systems that are required only on certain missions. While you can use them to good effect in combat situations, such tactics are difficult to master.

Every ship requires a transporter and a tractor beam, but if these systems are not vital to your mission or your style of play, you can replace the stock systems with type-I versions to conserve mass and improve performance. (For tactical information on the use of transporters and tractor beams in combat, see Chapter 3.)

Tables 8.15 and 8.16 show the mass and cost of all transporter and tractor beam systems.

	TRANSPORTER-I		TRANSPORTER-II		TRANSPORTER-III		TRANSPORTER-IV		TRANSPORTER-V	
	Mass	Cost	Mass	Cost	Mass	Cost	Mass	Cost	Mass	Cost
Federation	100	500	300	750	600	1,125	1,000	1,500	1,500	2,000
Klingon	100	500	325	750	650	1,125	1,100	1,500	1,650	2,000
Romulan	100	500	300	750	600	1,125	1,000	1,500	1,500	2,000
Borg	100	500	325	750	650	1,125	1,100	1,500	1,650	2,000

Table 8.15 Transporter Systems Mass and Cost

	TRANSPORTER-I		TRANSPORTER-II		TRANSPORTER-III		TRANSPORTER-IV		TRANSPORTER-V	
	Mass	Cost	Mass	Cost	Mass	Cost	Mass	Cost	Mass	Cost
Federation	100	500	300	750	600	1,125	1,000	1,500	1,500	2,000
Klingon	100	500	275	750	550	1,125	900	1,500	1,350	2,000
Romulan	100	500	275	750	550	1,125	900	1,500	1,350	2,000
Borg	100	500	325	750	650	1,125	1,100	1,500	1,650	2,000

Table 8.16 Tractor Beam Systems Mass and Cost

Bridge Systems

Bridge systems tend to be expensive prestige-wise, especially at the upper end of the spectrum. There are only two systems in this category—computers and cloaking devices—and only the computer is required.

Computers

Your computer controls your fire control and sensors. As such, it is a vital part of your ship. Never skimp on your computer to conserve mass. You should always install the best computer you can afford, since better computers provide better sensor range. If you expect to encounter cloaked enemies, a type-IV or -V computer (both of which have anticloak scan capability) is highly recommended.

Table 8.17 shows the mass and cost of all computer systems.

Bridge system attachment points (typical)

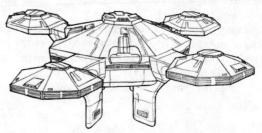

	COMPUTER-I		COMPUTER-II		COMPUTER-III		COMPUTER-IV		COMPUTER-V	
	Mass	Cost	Mass	Cost	Mass	Cost	Mass	Cost	Mass	Cost
Federation	100	500	200	750	300	1,130	500	2,000	700	3,000
Klingon	125	500	250	750	375	1,130	625	2,000	875	3,000
Romulan	100	550	200	830	300	1,250	500	2,500	700	3,750
Borg	125	500	250	750	375	1,125	625	2,000	875	3,000

Table 8.17 Computer Systems Mass and Cost

Cloaking Devices

Cloaking devices are *extremely* useful in *SFC3*. A cloak is standard equipment on every Klingon and Romulan ship. Take advantage of this system! If you need to save a little mass, downgrade the cloak. Unless you're really strapped for performance, *never* remove it. (Tactical information about the cloaking device can be found in Chapter 3.)

The mass and cost of each cloaking device is shown in Table 8.18.

	CLOAK-I		CLOAK-II		CLOAK-III		CLOAK-IV		CLOAK-V	
	Mass	Cost	Mass	Cost	Mass	Cost	Mass	Cost	Mass	Cost
Klingon	125	550	250	825	375	1,250	550	1,950	750	2,750
Romulan	100	500	200	750	350	1,125	500	1,750	700	2,500

Table 8.18 Cloaking Devices Mass and Cost

Engines

Engines serve three vital functions in your ship design: they provide maneuverability, combat speed, and power for all of your systems. As such, you cannot afford to sell your design short in any engine category. All three engine types are required equipment.

Engine attachment points
(typical)

Thrusters

Thrusters determine your ship's maneuverability. The more advanced the thruster system, the more maneuverable your ship. Turning ability is vital in *SFC3*, especially for ships with no aft firepower. If you can't bring your weapons to bear, you're out of luck. Make certain that your ship's mass doesn't overtax your thrusters, otherwise, you might as well christen your ship *USS Bull's-eye.*

Table 8.19a and 8.19b list the mass and cost of all thruster systems.

| | THRUSTER-I | | THRUSTER-II | | THRUSTER-III | | THRUSTER-IV | | THRUSTER-V | |
	Mass	Cost	Mass	Cost	Mass	Cost	Mass	Cost	Mass	Cost
Federation	375	250	475	350	600	450	800	550	1,000	650
Klingon	350	250	425	350	550	450	725	550	900	650
Romulan	350	250	425	350	550	450	725	550	900	650
Borg	425	250	500	340	675	425	875	515	1,100	605

Table 8.19a Thruster Types I–V Mass and Cost

| | THRUSTER-VI | | THRUSTER-VII | | THRUSTER-VIII | | THRUSTER-IX | | THRUSTER-X | |
	Mass	Cost	Mass	Cost	Mass	Cost	Mass	Cost	Mass	Cost
Federation	1,250	750	1,700	850	2,100	950	2,475	1,050	3,250	1,150
Klingon	1,250	750	1,525	850	1,900	950	2,225	1,050	2,925	1,150
Romulan	1,125	750	1,525	850	1,900	950	2,225	1,050	2,925	1,200
Borg	1,375	690	1,875	780	2,300	870	2,700	960	3,500	1,050

Table 8.19b Thruster Types VI–X Mass and Cost

Impulse Engines

Impulse engines determine your maximum speed in combat situations (warp jumps not with-standing). Just as it is easy to get carried away and out-mass your thrusters, it is possible to weigh down your ship enough that you lower your speed to a sub-light crawl by using an underpowered impulse engine. If you can't afford the mass and prestige of a more powerful impulse engine, shed some mass in other areas to keep your top speed as high as possible (20 or better is a good goal).

Table 8.20a and 8.20b show the mass and cost of all impulse engines.

| | IMPULSE-I | | IMPULSE-II | | IMPULSE-III | | IMPULSE-IV | | IMPULSE-V | |
	Mass	Cost	Mass	Cost	Mass	Cost	Mass	Cost	Mass	Cost
Federation	400	600	525	900	650	1,350	875	2,000	1,100	3,000
Klingon	500	665	625	1,000	750	1,500	1,000	2,200	1,250	3,300
Romulan	500	665	550	1,000	625	1,500	825	2,250	950	3,325
Borg	550	600	600	900	675	1,350	900	2,000	1,050	3,000

Table 8.20a Impulse Engine Types I–V Mass and Cost

| | IMPULSE-VI | | IMPULSE-VII | | IMPULSE-VIII | | IMPULSE-IX | | IMPULSE-X | |
	Mass	Cost	Mass	Cost	Mass	Cost	Mass	Cost	Mass	Cost
Federation	1,375	4,250	1,875	5,500	2,300	6,750	2,750	8,000	3,600	9,500
Klingon	1,500	4,700	1,750	6,000	2,200	7,500	2,500	8,750	3,250	10,500
Romulan	1,100	4,750	1,650	6,000	2,000	7,500	2,475	8,750	3,000	10,500
Borg	1,200	4,250	1,800	5,500	2,175	6,750	2,700	8,000	3,850	9,500

Table 8.20b Impulse Engine Types VI–X Mass and Cost

Warp Drive

Warp drive is your ship's power plant. It provides the energy for every system on your ship so, obviously, the better the warp drive, the more power you have at your disposal.

There is a vast array of warp engines to choose from, and each upgrade provides more power. Choose your warp engine last, after all of your other desired systems have been installed, and use the total warp power ratio to choose the engine that's right for you. If you can't balance your total warp power ratio with any of the engines you can afford (mass- or prestige-wise), that means you need to shed some of your other systems to compensate. It doesn't matter how many powerful weapons are bristling from your hull if you don't have enough power to charge them.

Tables 8.21a and 8.21b show the mass and cost of all warp drive systems.

	WARP-I		WARP-II		WARP-III		WARP-IV		WARP-V	
	Mass	Cost	Mass	Cost	Mass	Cost	Mass	Cost	Mass	Cost
Federation	800	3,000	1,050	3,650	1,300	4,325	1,750	5,400	2,200	6,500
Klingon	725	2,500	950	2,975	1,200	3,800	1,575	4,900	2,000	6,000
Romulan	900	3,250	1,150	3,775	1,450	4,320	1,925	4,995	2,400	5,940
Borg	800	2,975	1,050	3,650	1,300	4,325	1,750	5,400	2,200	6,475

Table 8.21a Warp Engine Types I–V Mass and Cost

	WARP-VI		WARP-VII		WARP-VIII		WARP-IX		WARP-X	
	Mass	Cost	Mass	Cost	Mass	Cost	Mass	Cost	Mass	Cost
Federation	2,750	8,100	3,750	9,725	4,600	11,500	5,500	13,500	7,200	19,600
Klingon	2,500	7,300	3,400	8,825	4,200	10,350	4,950	12,100	6,500	17,600
Romulan	3,000	7,425	4,100	9,585	5,000	11,880	6,000	14,175	7,900	19,575
Borg	2,750	8,100	3,750	10,800	4,600	12,950	5,500	15,400	7,200	19,600

Table 8.21b Warp Engine Types VI–X Mass and Cost

SHIPS ON A BUDGET

> **NOTE**
>
> The Borg have an eleventh type of warp drive, B-Warp-SB, which is used in their largest ships. It has a Mass of 10,700, and a cost of 30,000.

When you're designing ships for single-player skirmishes, the sky's the limit. Building ships without a prestige budget cap is a great way to test out new weapons and systems and get the feel for what it's like to pilot a nearly invulnerable ship that can beat anything in the galaxy.

When you're playing in the campaign or in a multiplayer game, however, you seldom have that kind of economic freedom. In these situations, you need to be able to build a good ship on a budget.

The following ships are examples of good, solid, custom ships created on a budget. (The prestige cost shown is the total prestige cost for the ship and all of its systems.) We'll concentrate on ship designs that fall well below the default 65,000-point limit set in skirmish games. (Expensive ships are easy. Efficient low-budget ships are the real challenge.)

Ships Under 30,000 Points

Norway Variant

Hull Class	Federation Norway
Shields	4 (F-Shield-III)
Primary Weapons	3 Fore (1 Phaser XF, 2 Phaser IXF)
Heavy Weapons	1 Fore (Photon Torpedo)
	1 Aft (Photon Torpedo)
Hull Systems	F-Tractor-I
	F-Armor-I
	F-Transporter-I
	Bridge Systems F-Computer-I
Engines	F-Thruster-I
	F-Impulse-I
	F-Warp-III

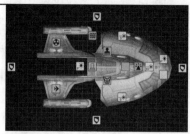

Federation *Norway* variant

K'Vort Variant

Hull Class	Klingon K'Vort
Shields	4 (K-Shield-III)
Primary Weapons	2 Fore (K-Disruptor II)
	1 Aft (K-Disruptor II)
Heavy Weapons	1 Fore (K-Photon Torpedo)
Hull Systems	K-Tractor-I
	K-Armor-I
	K-Transporter-I
Bridge Systems	K-Computer-I
	K-Cloak-I
Engines	K-Thruster-I
	K-Impulse-I
	K-Warp-III

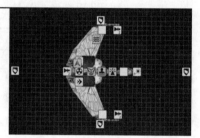

Klingon *K'Vort* variant

Falcon Variant

Hull Class	Romulan Falcon
Shields	4 (R-Shield-III)
Primary Weapons	3 Fore (3 R-Disruptor-II)
Heavy Weapons	1 Fore (Light Plasma Torpedo)
Hull Systems	R-Tractor-I
	R-Armor-II
	R-Transporter-I
Bridge Systems	R-Computer-I
	R-Cloak-I
Engines	R-Thruster-I
	R-Impulse-I
	R-Warp-III

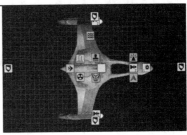

Romulan *Falcon* variant

Pyramid Prime Variant

Hull Class	Borg Pyramid Prime
Shields	N/A
Primary Weapons	1 Fore (Medium Cutting Beam-F)
	1 Port (Light Cutting Beam)
	1 Starboard (Light Cutting Beam)
	1 360-degree (Medium Cutting Beam-F)
Heavy Weapons	1 Fore (Gravametric Torpedo)
Hull Systems	B-Tractor-I
	B-Armor-II
	B-Transporter-I
Bridge Systems	B-Computer-I
Engines	B-Thruster-I
	B-Impulse-I
	B-Warp-II

Borg *Pyramid Prime* variant

37,000- to 50,000-Point Ships

Akira Variant

Hull Class	Federation Akira
Shields	4 (F-Shield-VI)
Primary Weapons	2 Fore (2 Phaser XF)
	1 Port (Phaser XF)
	1 Starboard (Phaser XF)
	1 360-degree (Phaser XF)
Heavy Weapons	2 Fore (2 Photon Torpedo)
	1 Aft (Photon Torpedo)
Hull Systems	F-Tractor-III
	F-Armor-II
	F-Transporter-II
Bridge Systems	F-Computer-II
Engines	F-Thruster-IV
	F-Impulse-IV
	F-Warp-VI

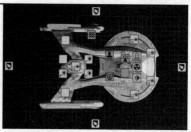

Federation *Akira* variant

K'Tinga Variant

Hull Class	Klingon K'Tinga
Shields	4 (3 K-Shield V, 1 K-Shield III aft)
Primary Weapons	2 Fore (2 Disruptor II)
	1 Port (Disruptor II)
	1 Starboard (Disruptor II)
	2 Aft (2 Disruptor II)
Heavy Weapons	1 Fore (K-Photon Torpedo)
	1 Aft (K-Photon Torpedo)
Hull Systems	K-Tractor-II
	K-Armor-III
	K-Transporter-I
Bridge Systems	K-Computer-I
	K-Cloak-I
Engines	K-Thruster-II
	K-Impulse-I
	K-Warp-VI

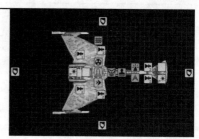

Klingon *K'Tinga* variant

Chapter 8: Space Dock—Starship Design

Hawk Variant

Hull Class	Romulan Hawk
Shields	4 (R-Shield-VI forward, 3 R-Shield-V)
Primary Weapons	3 Fore (3 R-Disruptor II)
	1 Port (R-Disruptor II)
	1 Starboard (R-Disruptor II)
	2 Aft (R-Disruptor I)
Heavy Weapons	2 Fore (2 Medium Plasma Torpedoes)
Hull Systems	R-Tractor-III
	R-Armor-III
	R-Transporter-III
Bridge Systems	R-Computer-III
	R-Cloak-I
Engines	R-Thruster-III
	R-Impulse-III
	R-Warp-VII

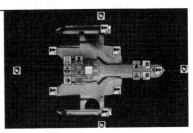

Romulan *Hawk* variant

Sphere Prime Variant

Hull Class	Borg Sphere Prime
Shields	N/A
Primary Weapons	1 Fore (Medium Cutting Beam)
	1 Port (Medium Cutting Beam)
	1 Starboard (Medium Cutting Beam)
	1 Aft (Medium Cutting Beam)
	2 360-degree (Medium Cutting Beam-F)
Heavy Weapons	1 Fore (Gravametric Torpedo)
	1 Port (Gravametric Torpedo)
	1 Starboard (Gravametric Torpedo)
	1 Aft (Gravametric Torpedo)
Hull Systems	B-Tractor-III
	B-Armor-III
	B-Transporter-I
Bridge Systems	B-Computer-IV
Engines	B-Thruster-V
	B-Impulse-V
	B-Warp-VII

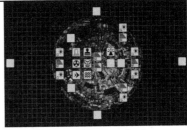

Borg *Sphere Prime* variant

SHIPS OF THE LINE

If you're a true *Star Trek* fan, the ability to create custom starships probably has you itching to recreate some of the ships that have been seen in the television shows and feature films. The following sections provide you with the specifications you need to create several of the most famous *Star Trek* vessels, based on the statistics available in the official *Star Trek* reference volumes and the ships' observed behavior in the movies and television shows.

USS *Enterprise* (NCC-1701D)

The Galaxy-class *USS Enterprise* served as the Federation flagship from her launch in 2363 until her destruction at Veridian III in 2371.

USS Enterprise (NCC-1701D) Specifications

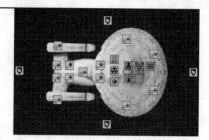

Hull Class	Federation Galaxy
Shields	4 (F-Shield-VIII)
Primary Weapons	2 Fore (2 Phaser XS)
	2 Port (2 Phaser XS)
	2 Starboard (2 Phaser XS)
	2 Aft (2 Phaser IXS)
	1 360 degree (Phaser XF)
Heavy Weapons	2 Fore (2 Photon Torpedoes)
	2 Aft (2 Photon Torpedoes)
Hull Systems	F-Tractor-IV
	F-Armor-III
	F-Transporter-IV
Bridge Systems	F-Computer-IV
Engines	F-Thruster-VI
	F-Impulse-VI
	F-Warp-VIII

USS Enterprise (NCC-1701E)

Launched in 2372, the Sovereign-class *USS Enterprise* was the seventh starship to bear the name. The *Enterprise-E*, under the command of Captain Jean-Luc Picard, played a pivotal role in repelling a Borg invasion of Earth in 2373.

USS Enterprise (NCC-1701E) Specifications

Hull Class	Federation Sovereign
Shields	4 (F-Shield-X)
Primary Weapons	2 Fore (2 Phaser XIF)
	1 Port (Phaser XIF)
	1 Starboard (2 Phaser XIF)
	2 Aft (2 Phaser XIF)
Heavy Weapons	3 Fore (2 Quantum Torpedoes, 1 Photon Torpedo)
	1 Aft (1 Photon Torpedo)
Hull Systems	F-Tractor-V
	F-Armor-IV
	F-Transporter-III
Bridge Systems	F-Computer-V
Engines	F-Thruster-V
	F-Impulse-V
	F-Warp-X

USS Voyager (NCC-74656)

While hunting for Maquis raiders in the Badlands in 2371, the *USS Voyager* was propelled into the Delta Quadrant, 70,000 light-years from Federation space. She was presumed destroyed until 2374, when the ship's Emergency Medical Hologram managed to get a message through to Starfleet. *Voyager* returned safely to the Alpha Quadrant in 2378.

USS Voyager Specifications

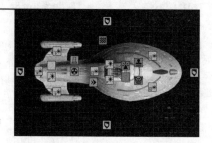

Hull Class	Federation Intrepid
Shields	4 (F-Shield-IV)
Primary Weapons	2 Fore (2 Phaser XS)
	1 Port (Phaser IXS)
	1 Starboard (Phaser IXS)
	1 Aft (Phaser IXS)
	1 360 degree (Phaser XF)
Heavy Weapons	2 Fore (2 Photon Torpedoes)
	1 Aft (1 Photon Torpedo)
Hull Systems	F-Tractor-III
	F-Armor-III
	F-Transporter-II
Bridge Systems	F-Computer-II
Engines	F-Thruster-III
	F-Impulse-III
	F-Warp-VI

USS Defiant (NX-74205)

Originally designed to combat the Borg, the *USS Defiant* was assigned to Federation outpost Deep Space Nine in 2371 to guard against Dominion incursions into the Alpha Quadrant. The original ship was destroyed in 2375 and was replaced by the *USS Sao Paulo* (which was given the *Defiant's* name and registry number).

USS Defiant Specifications

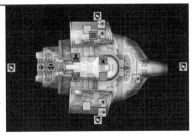

Hull Class	Federation Defiant
Shields	4 (F-Shield IV forward, 3 F-Shield-III)
Primary Weapons	3 Fore (2 Pulse Phaser, 1 Phaser IXF)
Heavy Weapons	2 Fore
	(1 Quantum Torpedo, 1 Photon Torpedo)
Hull Systems	F-Tractor-I
	F-Armor-IV
	F-Transporter-I
Bridge Systems	F-Computer-III
Engines	F-Thruster-V
	F-Impulse-IV
	F-Warp-IV

NOTE

The Defiant *shown here is the post-2375 configuration. After the end of the Dominion War, the Romulans apparently forced the Federation to remove the* Defiant's *borrowed cloaking device. (In other words, there's no way to put a cloaking device on a Federation ship in* SFC3.*)*

I.K.V. Rotarran

The *I.K.V. Rotarran*, under command of General Martok, served the allied fleet throughout the Dominion War. The *Rotarran* was part of the combined Federation and Klingon taskforce that retook Deep Space Nine after the station was captured by the Dominion in 2374.

I.K.V. Rotarran Specifications

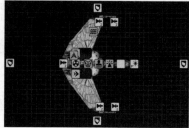

Hull Class	Klingon K'Vort
Shields	4 (K-Shield-IV forward, 2 K-Shield-III port and starboard, 1 K-Shield-II aft)
Primary Weapons	4 Fore (4 Disruptor II)
	1 Aft (Disruptor II)
Heavy Weapons	1 Fore (K-Photon Torpedo)
Hull Systems	K-Tractor-II
	K-Armor-III
	K-Transporter-I
Bridge Systems	K-Computer-I
	K-Cloak-I
Engines	K-Thruster-I
	K-Impulse-I
	K-Warp-IV

9

Command Decisions

Your split-second decisions, power- and weapon-management skills, and superior reflexes are what make you shine during a mission. In a campaign, however, effective starship command skills extend beyond the heat-of-the-moment combat training you've spent so much time honing and perfecting. The decisions you make and actions you take before and after campaign missions have a profound effect on your ability to cope with the situations you encounter in the missions themselves.

In this chapter, we'll take a look at what you do between missions in a campaign and how those pre- and post-mission actions and decisions affect the outcome of individual missions and the campaign as a whole.

EXPLORING THE GALAXY

The galactic map is more than just an overview of who controls which sectors (hexes) or a convenient interface for moving across great distances. It's actually your long-range sensor array, which provides you with the location of certain objects and phenomena in the surrounding sectors and monitors enemy ship locations and fleet movements (see Figure 9.1).

Figure 9.1 The galactic map—a wealth of information at your cursor tip.

Environmental Factors

Although space is mostly empty, there are many environmental factors that can affect your missions in certain sectors. Many of these elements—such as asteroid fields, planets, black holes, nebulae, and enemy bases—are clearly marked on the galactic map (see Figure 9.2).

The type of environment that exists in a sector can greatly affect your combat tactics (see Chapter 3 for details). To avoid surprises, check the local conditions on the map before you enter a mission.

Enemy Activity

A quick glance at the galactic map might make you believe that the game is frozen when you're not in combat. Nothing could be further from the truth! Things are happening all the time—you just don't always see them.

A savvy commander uses the galactic map to monitor enemy activity before plotting their course. You can scan any adjacent map sector by right-clicking it. The most important information you gain from a scan is whether or not enemy vessels occupy the sector. Ships or groups thereof appear as squares that show the ship type and are color-coded to match the various empires (red for Klingon, blue for Federation, green for Romulan). When you actually perform a scan, the names, captains, and vessel types appear in the information window below the map.

When you spot a ship and sit still long enough, you can see that the map is indeed in motion. Ships are moving to and fro all the time (see Figures 9.3 and 9.4).

By keeping an eye on enemy ship movements in adjacent sectors, you can plot your course around them to avoid an attack—or select a ripe target to kill for some extra prestige points.

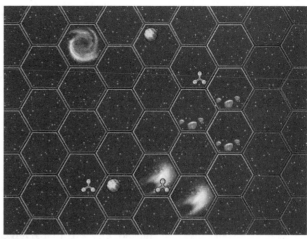

Figure 9.2 Check the map for environmental conditions before moving from sector to sector so you know what to expect.

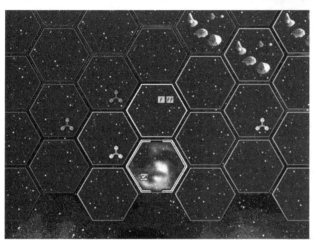

Figure 9.3 A Klingon frigate and freighter convoy on the move from one adjacent sector...

NOTE

You can also see what's going on in the big galactic picture by clicking the News button. The news feed, which is updated periodically, shows you what's happening in the sectors that aren't close enough to scan.

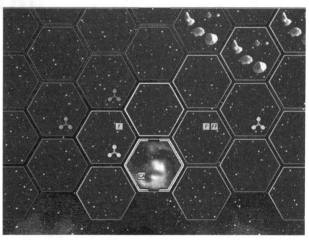

Figure 9.4 ...to another. The galactic map is constantly in motion.

Non-Core Missions

Whenever you enter a new sector, check your Missions button to see if it's active. When it is, you have the opportunity to engage in non-core campaign missions that add to your prestige and provide valuable practice for upcoming critical engagements.

For details on the types of campaign missions you can participate in between the core missions that are assigned to you, see Chapter 13.

PRESTIGE

Every mission you successfully complete adds to your prestige. In *SFC3*, prestige not only determines your rank and status in the game, but also acts as a form of currency that you use to upgrade and supply your existing ship or to purchase new ships.

Your prestige is tracked only within a given campaign. For example, when you're playing the Klingon campaign, your prestige accrues from mission to mission right up until you complete the entire campaign—and that's it. When you start the Romulan campaign, your prestige total restarts at 100 (the starting prestige for every campaign).

WARNING

You have a certain amount of latitude time-wise when proceeding to an assigned (core) campaign mission. That means you have time for one or perhaps two non-core missions on your way. Eventually, you're forced to comply with your orders and proceed to your assigned sector and, once there, you cannot leave until you have completed the core mission in that location.

Since you can't take your prestige with you from campaign to campaign, you might as well use it along the way. Upgrade your ship as often as you can, and when you can afford it, buy a new, larger ship. You deserve the best, and in many cases, you can't effectively go beyond a certain point in a campaign without a bigger ship. (See the mission descriptions in Chapters 10–12 for suggestions on when to switch vessels.)

Promotions and Awards

Prestige is also used to track your rank and standing in the service of your empire's fleet. Promotions are awarded as you reach certain levels of prestige. Don't worry: spending prestige on ships and supplies doesn't mean that you're forestalling your promotion. The game tracks your lifetime prestige total separately from your current prestige "bank account." (You can't see it, but it's there.)

Prestige and Communications

Most core campaign missions have a great deal of communications dialogue—between you and your officers or between you and enemies or allies on other ships in the area.

You might be tempted to click through the comm exchanges without thinking to get the mission rolling, but this is a bad idea. Making the correct dialogue choices in some exchanges can score you extra prestige points—but some dialogue choices can subtract from your score. See the "Dialogue Prestige" section of each mission's overview in Chapters 10–12 for a list of the dialogue choices that affect prestige in each core mission.

When you complete certain missions, you have the chance of being awarded medals and commendations for demonstrating your command prowess. Each mission medal and special commendation you win is a mark of distinction on your campaign record (see Figure 9.5).

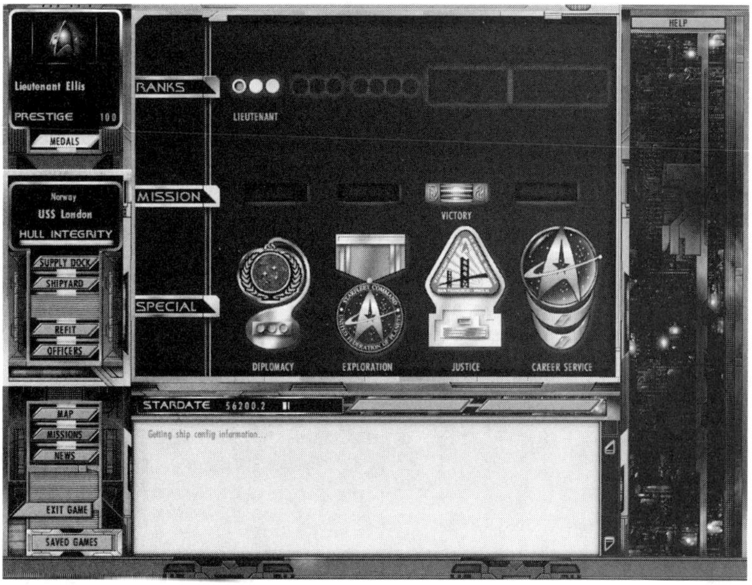

SPACE DOCK

Of all the between-mission activities available, visiting space dock is easily the most important. As a starship captain, you're expected to handle most situations autonomously. If your luck holds, you might go through several missions without needing to head home, but there are times when you have no choice but to visit a friendly space dock.

Figure 9.5 Your trophy case—the rewards of a successful career as a starship commander

Repairing Your Ship

System repairs that you don't complete in battle are taken care of automatically when you move into a sector that contains a friendly base. Hull repairs, on the other hand, require an actual visit to space dock.

To repair your hull, go to the Supply screen (see Figure 9.6). The prestige cost for the repair is shown at the top of the screen. Click the Repair button to bring your hull back to like-new condition.

Whenever your hull has been damaged, make a post-mission detour to the nearest base your top priority. Ships with low hull integrity don't survive long in intense combat.

NOTE

A "friendly" space dock is any base facility on the map that belongs to an empire you're not at war with. Federation ships can visit Klingon bases for repairs and refits as needed, and vice versa.

Restocking Your Ship

Another good reason to visit a base after a combat mission is to restock supplies. In *SFC3*, your supply manifest comprises shuttlecraft, marines, and mines. If you've used any of these expendable resources, visit the Supply screen and load up. Always max out your stores. The usefulness of shuttles, marines, and mines far outweigh their negligible cost.

NOTE

Starfleet Command *veterans will notice that supplying ships has been greatly simplified in SFC3. It's particularly important to note that you no longer have to buy spare parts for your ship. Your parts storage is automatically refilled to capacity at the start of every new mission.*

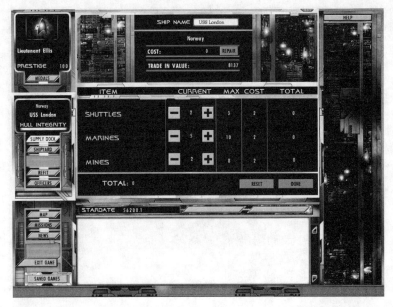

Figure 9.6 If you have enough prestige, repair is just a click away.

Refitting Your Ship

In the previous *Starfleet Command* games, "refitting" your ship was as easy as buying a new starship in the same class that had a better— or at least different—weapon configuration. In *SFC3*, you must take on the role of starship designer and upgrade your ship's systems and weapons yourself (see Figure 9.7).

When you first take command, your ship is always in its default configuration. In most cases, the default weapons and systems don't take full advantage of the ship's potential. By spending a little creativity and prestige, you can greatly improve your ship's combat performance and survivability. Prestige is your currency in *SFC3*. You can't take it with you from campaign to campaign, so you might as well put it to good use. When you can't afford to buy a new ship, make the most of your existing one.

For detailed information on refitting and redesigning ships, see Chapter 8.

TIP

Sometimes refitting your existing ship is preferable to upgrading to a bigger one. If after you buy a larger ship, you have no prestige left to tweak the new ship's weapons and systems, you might be better off maxing your current loadout and sticking with your current command until you accumulate a little more prestige. A good example is upgrading from a Federation Intrepid-class light cruiser to an Akira-class heavy cruiser. If you can't upgrade the Akira's weaponry and improve on its default firing arcs immediately after buying it, you're better off adding more (or better) weapons and systems to your Intrepid.

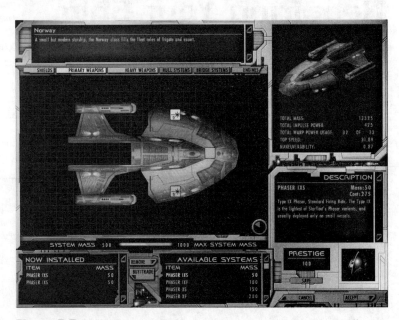

Figure 9.7 Visit the ship Refit screen to improve your vessel's combat performance.

Replacing Your Ship

When you accumulate a huge amount of prestige, it's time to start thinking about leaving your current ship behind and picking up something bigger and more powerful. When you visit the Shipyard screen, you can have a look at what's available (see Figure 9.8). Ships you can't afford are grayed out. Remember that your current ship has a trade-in value (which is shown at the top of the Supply screen), so you don't need to accumulate enough prestige for the full price of the ship, just enough so that your prestige plus your current ship's trade-in value is equal to or higher than the new ship's price.

As you progress through the campaign, you should upgrade to a larger ship whenever you have enough prestige to afford it. (See

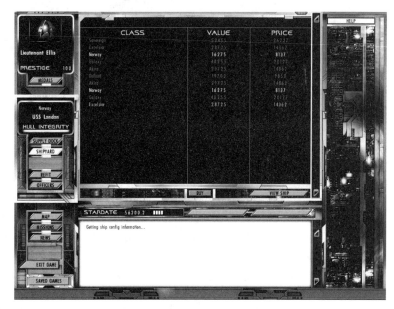

Figure 9.8 Time for a new ship.

the tip in the previous section for a caveat to this practice.) Missions get progressively harder, and only the biggest, most powerful starships can survive the beating you'll take in the climactic encounters of each campaign. The ships available during campaign games are described in Chapters 4–7.

If you're particularly wealthy prestige-wise, you might notice that large facilities, such as battlestations and starbases, appear on your list of available ships. You can purchase these facilities and place them in any friendly sector that currently has no base. Do this by moving into the empty sector, clicking the Missions button, and selecting the Deliver Starbase mission from the mission list. This mission is automatic. The base appears on the map without your having to enter the combat portion of the game.

Adding a new starbase to an empty region of your empire provides a convenient rest stop. A base near the enemy front means you don't have to cross half your empire to repair and re-supply your ship after battle. Because bases are so expensive, however, you should consider spending the prestige on one only when you already have the best ship you can afford.

NOTE

Avoid confrontations until after you deliver your newly purchased base. If you have purchased a new base and are killed in combat before you deliver it, the base is lost along with your ship.

Recruiting Your Crew

As the captain, you're responsible for most of your own actions. There are, however, many shipboard tasks that are out of your control. Your crew handles these tasks.

In *SFC3*, your command crew is made up of six individuals, each with a specific set of duties to perform:

Tactical: The officer that targets and fires your weapons. The more skilled your tactical officer, the better chance you have of hitting an enemy when you fire. Good tactical officers can also increase weapon damage yield and accurately target subsystems on the target vessel.

Helm: Your ship's pilot. Your helmsman's skill determines whether or not you can perform complex maneuvers such as high-energy turns and, if so, how well those maneuvers are performed.

Security: The officer who trains your marines and directs them when boarding other vessels and defending your ship from enemy boarding parties. The better your security officer, the higher your success rate in marine raids and capture attempts against other ships and defending your ship from the same.

Ops: The officer who handles your scanners. A good ops officer scans targets faster, has a better chance of detecting enemy ships with an anticloak scan, and can find weaknesses in enemy ships.

Engineering: The officer who monitors your engine efficiency and repairs damaged systems. A good engineer can get extra speed out of your impulse engines, extra power out of your warp drive, and repair damaged systems quickly and efficiently.

Medical: The officer who heals injured crewmembers (most notably members of your command crew).

When one of your officers is injured or killed in battle, the others fill in as best they can, but your ship's performance efficiency in the functions under the injured officer's purview is severely affected.

Each member of your command crew has a set of three basic statistics and 18 specific skills that define how well they perform their duties. (These statistics are described in the game manual.) You can check your crew's statistics in the left column of the Officers screen (see Figure 9.9). From this screen you can also recruit replacements when you lose officers in battle or when your current command crew isn't performing to your satisfaction.

Every member of your command crew can learn all 18 skills. Their level of competence in each is defined as follows, from least to most competent:

1. Basic

2. Trained

3. Skilled

4. Veteran

5. Expert

6. Legendary

You can personally assign each officer to a given position, or you can use the Auto Assign feature to have the computer assign your crew to their optimum positions based on their skill ratings. The Auto Assign works really well and is the recommended method for crew assignment.

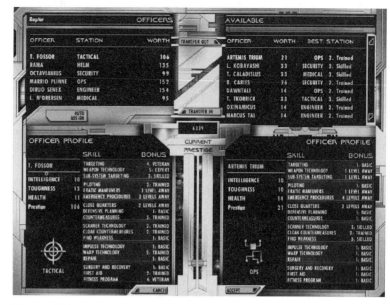

Figure 9.9 Monitor your command-crew status and recruit new crewmembers on the Officers screen.

As mentioned earlier, you can transfer any or all members of your command crew at any time and replace them with new crewmembers when you're at a friendly base. Like everything else, this costs prestige. The amount of prestige each crewmember "costs" is based on the officer's overall skill level.

If you're going to make crew changes, make them early on and stick with the same crew throughout the campaign. As you complete missions, your crew becomes more skilled in their respective positions. The replacement officers available at your bases are invariably less skilled than your current crew if you've successfully completed several missions together. When an officer gains skill in battle, this is noted on the information display under the galactic map as soon as you exit the mission.

10

The Klingon Campaign

The single-player campaign in *Starfleet Command III* is divided into three parts, each of which revolves around one of the three major empires. You can play the campaign segments in whatever order you prefer, but since the campaign is meant to tell a story, you should consider playing them in the order designed:

1. Klingon
2. Romulan
3. Federation

This chapter provides a walkthrough for each of the 15 core missions in the Klingon campaign. The campaign progression is linear, and you must complete each core mission to continue. If you fail any mission, the campaign ends and you lose.

MISSION 1—BROTHERHOOD

"You have sided against us in battle, and this we do not forgive...or forget."—Gowron

Mission Briefing

We are on patrol in the Girthrin Sector, a volatile area along the Romulan-Klingon Neutral Zone. As this is my first command, I am serving under the guidance and tutelage of my older brother Jureth, the leader of our House's finest squadron. While the patrol has been uneventful, it has been good to serve alongside my brother and other members of the house of Mi'Qogh. Our squadron is to keep an eye on the Girthrin system, where our outpost worlds share a star system with the Romulans, with our forces in uncomfortable proximity to each other. We shall be vigilant for the slightest sign of trouble.

Mission Overview

Objectives	Patrol area with Jureth.
	Follow Jureth's lead.
Environment	Scattered Asteroids; Planets
Basic Mission Prestige	1,000
Bonus Prestige	+ 300 for each Romulan ship captured
Dialogue Prestige	"Dull my senses?..." (-10)
	"It is an honor..." (+50)

Shortly after you enter the sector, two Romulan warships appear near the planet. Follow Jureth's lead and engage the Romulans. Because Jureth's ship is the bigger threat, the Romulans concentrate on him—which leaves you plenty of breathing room.

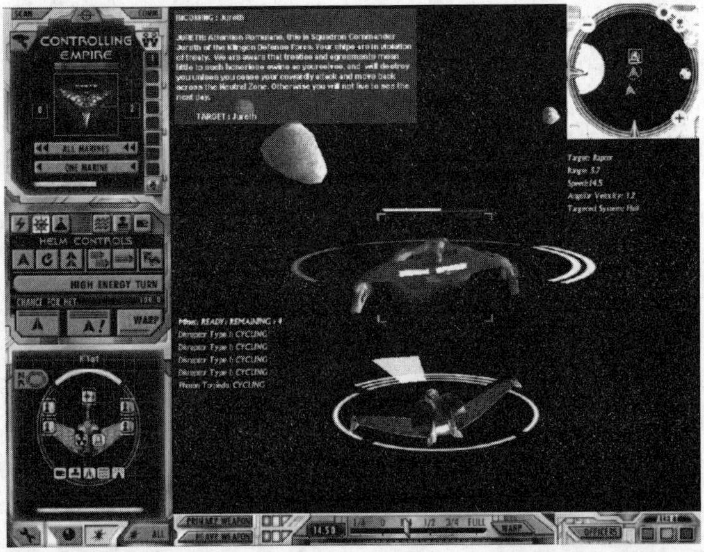

You can win the mission by either destroying or capturing the Romulan ships. Focus on the smaller ship first—you're no match for the larger one. Make capture your goal. It's fairly easy to capture the smaller Romulan ship, and you can use the extra firepower when dealing with its larger companion. As soon as you get their shields down, start beaming over marines. You need to get as many marines in place as you can as quickly as possible because Jureth is shooting to kill (although he will beam some of his marines over as well).

After you deal with the small ship, turn your attention to the larger one. Use your cloaking device and your superior maneuverability to stay

Figure 10.1 Stay well away from the large Romulan's forward weapons if you want to survive.

behind the Romulan, out of his forward weapons arc. Your ship is too small to handle that kind of firepower (see Figure 10.1). Capturing this ship isn't as easy as capturing the smaller one, but you should try. The extra prestige will come in handy down the line.

TIP

Before you start the mission, make sure you stock up on marines. You can score a lot of extra prestige points by capturing the Romulan ships rather than destroying them.

MISSION 2— A VAST YE SCURVY TARGS

Mission Briefing

Imperial Intelligence reports increasing acts of piracy in your sector. We will not tolerate piracy against either the Empire or the House of Mi'Qogh. Your orders are to exterminate all pirate activity in the area!

Mission Overview

Objectives	Destroy or capture pirates in area.
Environment	Open Space; Dust Cloud
Basic Mission Prestige	1,000
Bonus Prestige	+ 100 for each ship captured
Dialogue Prestige	None

When the mission begins, immediately engage the pirate frigate. This shouldn't be too much of a problem—you easily outgun the enemy. Try to capture the ship if possible—the extra prestige comes in handy. The pirate has no aft weapons so, if you stay behind him, you're safe.

Notice how the pirate isn't engaging the supposedly beleaguered freighter? This is significant. The freighter is actually under pirate control. As soon as the pirate frigate's condition is critical, the freighter starts taking pot shots at you (see Figure 10.2). After you've dealt with the frigate, wipe out the freighter. The freighter's disruptor fires in almost any direction, so prepare to take a couple of hits.

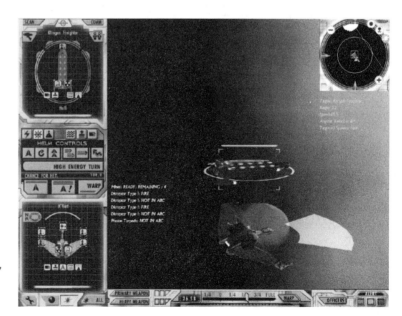

Figure 10.2 The freighter you're attempting to rescue is actually under pirate control.

MISSION 3— A BASE TOO FAR

Mission Briefing

A band of alien prisoners at the Krolom-792 mining facility have launched an uprising and are now in control of the station. The station governor and many members of the security garrison have been killed, and the prisoners now hold a number of Klingon workers hostage. They are also in control of an ore freighter that was docked at the station. We must ruthlessly quash this rebellion or risk seeing it spread. The Krolom-792 facility is a valuable asset of our house and we cannot afford to see it destroyed.

Mission Overview

Objectives	Recapture the base.
	Recapture the freighter.
Environment	Asteroid Field; Hostile Klingon Asteroid Base
Basic Mission Prestige	2,050
Bonus Prestige	+100 for capturing the base
	+50 for capturing the freighter
Dialogue Prestige	None

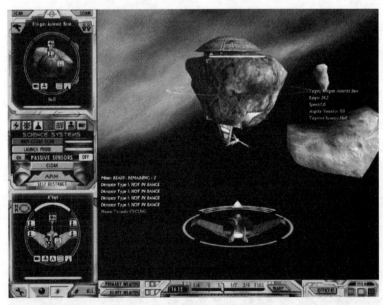

Figure 10.3 You must make several close passes at the asteroid base to transport your marines aboard.

If you want to maximize your prestige, you need to recapture the freighter before you take the base. Move into attack range and knock down the freighter's shields as quickly as possible. The freighter is armed, of course, but your biggest concern is the type-V disruptor on the asteroid base. You're well within its range when you're dealing with the freighter. Don't expend more than four marines on the freighter; you need at least six to recapture the base. You can lose the freighter and still complete the mission, but if you lose the base, the mission cannot succeed.

After the freighter is out of the way, it's time to hit the base. The asteroid base has 360-degree weapons, so there's no way to escape them. Take down one of the base's shields and set a tight circular course, keeping the shield facing the base reinforced at all times if possible. Wait for the base to fire. Then, while the base's weapons are recycling, move in to range 5 and transport marines into the base (see Figure 10.3). Repeat this until you have enough marines aboard to recapture the station. The mission ends immediately after the station is recaptured, which is why you have to capture the freighter first to get those bonus prestige points.

MISSION 4—SEARCH AND RESCUE

Mission Briefing

My Lord, Fleet Command sends word that they have lost contact with one of our vessels, *IKV Firebrand*. We have reached the Spire Nebula. The last known position of our ship was near here.

Mission Overview

Objectives	Investigate missing ship.
Environment	Nebula
Basic Mission Prestige	2,000
Bonus Prestige	None
Dialogue Prestige	None

When the mission begins, the missing ship is nowhere to be seen. Set course roughly toward the center of the map and proceed at half-impulse. You should locate the vessel fairly quickly.

Pirates have captured the missing vessel. It attacks you as soon as the pirate captain is finished taunting and you enter weapons range. Engage the enemy and fire at will, staying out of the opposing ship's weapon arcs when possible. Because the battle takes place in a nebula, you cannot use your transporters to send in the marines to recapture the ship. You have no recourse but to destroy the vessel (see Figure 10.4).

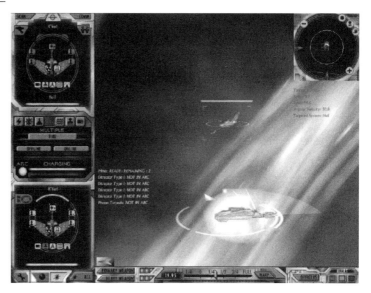

Figure 10.4 The missing vessel is under pirate control, and you must destroy it to complete the mission.

115

MISSION 5— WINDS OF CHANGE

Mission Briefing

We are being relieved at Girthrin by Admiral Khokit's Rapid Reaction fleet. We have been ordered to proceed to the Adeptus system, near the Federation border. There are two M-class planets there with a large asteroid field in the area. We are to be briefed there as to our role in support of the new Unity space station…a triumph of Klingon and Federation science, and a tribute to the Alliance between our two governments, long may it last.

Mission Overview

Objectives	Deliver two freighters to a base near the Federation border.
Environment	Asteroid Field; Planets;
Basic Mission Prestige	1,800
Bonus Prestige	+ 50 for each Rakellian vessel destroyed (first wave)
	+ 100 for each Rakellian vessel captured (first wave)
	+ 50 for each Rakellian captured (second wave)
Dialogue Prestige	"My family has counseled me…" (+10)
	"Yes, I think that we could spare some…" (+75)

The freighters you're meant to escort are on the far side of the map, across the asteroid field. Don't make a mistake and follow the freighters that are near your starting position. They'll lead you off the map and you'll fail the mission. Set course for the freighters and head into the asteroid field.

When you enter the asteroid field, several Rakellian vessels ambush you. Keep your speed low.

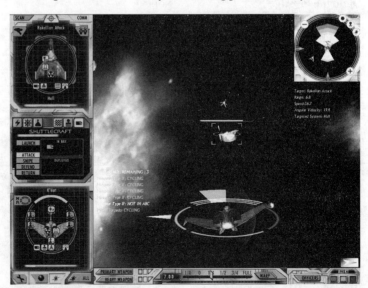

Figure 10.5 Try to lure the first wave of Rakellians into open space rather than fighting them in the asteroid field.

WARNING

If the first group of Rakellians doesn't detect you—if you're cloaked when you enter the asteroid field, for example—then make a beeline for the freighters and open fire on them. You must engage this first wave of enemies on the near side of the asteroid field if possible to keep the freighters safe for the time being.

You don't want to slam into any asteroids while you're engaged in combat! Turn around and leave the asteroid field when you detect the enemy ships. With some luck, they might follow you into open space (see Figure 10.5). After dispatching the first wave of enemies, rendezvous with the freighters.

While escorting the freighters through the asteroid field, a second wave of Rakellians that's led by a light cruiser ambushes the freighters. Both freighters must survive to complete the mission. Since you're outnumbered, don't waste time trying to capture the ships. Take them out as quickly as possible.

TIP

Rakellian vessels—your enemies in this mission—are small and fast. You need weapons that can strike for a maximum amount of damage in a single volley because these ships won't stay in your sights for long. Upgrade to type-II disruptors in a couple of your mounts (if possible) before you begin the mission.

MISSION 6— ANVIL OF PEACE

Mission Briefing

We have successfully escorted the supply freighters to the designated coordinates. Here at the Unity Starbase, we will beam down Ambassador Marketh to meet with the humans. It will be good to be rid of the Ambassador, whose inane chatter and propensity for questioning my orders under his breath—on my own bridge—have caused me to reach for my *d'k'tagh* several times on this voyage.

Mission Overview

Objectives	Follow the orders of the Federation commander.
	Deliver the Ambassador.
Environment	Asteroid Field; Unity Starbase
Basic Mission Prestige	1,800
Bonus Prestige	+100 for forcing the Romulan leave without a fight
	+ 10 for destroying the Romulan ship
	+10 for capturing the Romulan ship
	+50 for each Rakellian ship destroyed
	+75 for each Rakellian ship captured
Dialogue Prestige	**To Picard:**
	"We appreciate the welcome…" (+5)
	"Spare me your human pleasantries…" (-5)
	"Although we Klingons enjoy…" (+5)
	To the Romulans:
	"My weapons shall do…" (-10)
	"There is no explanation required…" (+10)
	"Romulan, do not annoy…" (+5)
	To the Ferengi:
	"Ah, the Ferengi…" (+10)

After your conversation with Picard, warp to the starbase and drop off the Ambassador. Proceed to the asteroid field when you're ordered to do so (turn left at the starbase from your initial heading). When the Romulan vessel decloaks, your best (and most profitable) course of action is to talk them out of fighting. Say the right things and the Romulans go away. (See Dialogue Prestige in the Mission Overview for a hint.)

Immediately after the Romulans depart, you receive a message about incoming Rakellians. Their target is the starbase, so warp to the base to intercept them. The Rakellian ships are small, so if you keep them near the base, the base's weapons help you tear them apart in no time.

When the Ferengi arrive, just navigate the comm dialogue to complete the mission.

MISSION 7— TURNING THE TABLES

Mission Briefing

I see that you have successfully completed your escort mission to Unity. I understand that we now have the location of a Rakellian base, in the Fessari B system. It goes without saying that we will not let this facility spend very many more hours in one piece. Command of the assault force that will annihilate these criminals will offer a perfect test of your warrior skills.

Complete this mission with the utmost courage, and I may appoint you additional ships to command in future missions. You should see to the repair and re-arming of your ship before you go on the offensive. Like the poet Kamahl of Vokron said, "Nothing cuts so fiercely as an over-sharpened blade." Let not a single Rakellian coward remain on that rock.

Mission Overview

Objectives	Destroy the Rakellian Asteroid Base
Environment	Asteroid Field; Rakellian Asteroid Base; Rakellian Defense Platforms
Basic Mission Prestige	2,000
Bonus Prestige	+100 for capturing the base
	+50 for each attack ship destroyed
	+75 for each attack ship captured
	+100 for sending fake message
	+ 100 for each light cruiser destroyed
	+150 for each light cruiser captured
	+300 for completing mission without Jureth's assistance
Dialogue Prestige	None

As you're following the arrow toward the asteroid base, Rakellian attack ships ambush you from the asteroids to your right. Deal with them before you proceed, luring them outside the asteroid field if possible before you engage (it's safer that way). You and your squadron should make fast work of them. Don't take too long, though. The ships covering the asteroid base join the fight if you don't dispatch the initial wave quickly.

It behooves you to capture at least one of the enemy ships. If you do so, you can send out a fake distress call to the asteroid base that causes some or all of the ships that are protecting the base to leave the sector. When prompted by the incoming communication, order the captured ship to the base. Order your squad to cloak and approach slowly so that you aren't detected during the time between the message's transmission and the departure of the enemy ships.

After you receive the message that the enemy has taken the bait, decloak and fire at will. You need to destroy or capture the asteroid base and eliminate the base and all Rakellian ships (but not the weapons platforms) to complete the mission.

MISSION 8— FISH IN A BARREL

> ## WARNING
>
> *Make sure you're well away from the stardocks when they explode. Even at a range of 10, the explosion is strong enough to inflict serious damage.*

Mission Briefing

We are dropping out of warp speed now. We have entered the Kholna'ch system. Our long-range probes have located several Rakellian space docks in the vicinity.

Mission Overview

Objectives	Destroy all Rakellian space docks and any defenders.
Environment	Open Space; Planet; Star
Basic Mission Prestige	2,000
Bonus Prestige	+25 for each Rakellian ship captured
Dialogue Prestige	None

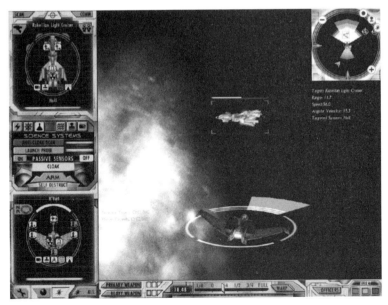

The Rakellian space docks are in orbit of the planet directly ahead. Cloak and approach at war speed. The docks themselves are unarmed, but they're protected by Rakellian attack ships and light cruisers. Take out the defenders first, starting with the larger ships (see Figure 10.6).

After the defending vessels are out of the way, this mission lives up to its name. The stardocks are completely defenseless, so you can take them out at your leisure.

Figure 10.6 Take out the defending ships before you attack the stardocks.

MISSION 9— OBEDIENCE

Mission Briefing

Ship's Log, supplemental. Jureth's intelligence officer has tipped me off to a Rakellian convoy attempting to move one of their outpost facilities to a safer location. We will attempt to intercept this convoy before it enters the Viper's Head Nebula. Destroying it will help rid the Empire of a politically volatile nuisance on our border with the Federation.

Mission Overview

Objectives	Catch and destroy Rakellian convoy.
Environment	Nebula; Asteroid Field
Basic Mission Prestige	2,000
Bonus Prestige	+25 for each attack ship destroyed
	+50 for each attack ship captured
Dialogue Prestige	**To Rakelli escort:**
	"No, we will not violate our moral code…" (+200)
	To Rakelli freighter:
	"You are beaten!…" (+100)
	To Jureth:
	"As you wish, brother." (-100)

The Rakellian freighters are dead ahead. Set a course for them and get underway immediately. This is a timed mission. The convoy is already on the other side of the asteroid field and making for the edge of the sector. Target the most distant freighter and deal with it first. Don't waste time dealing with the escort. Your priority is the freighters.

After you take out the two most distant freighters, Jureth contacts you. Follow the dialog path of your choice. There is no need to destroy the remaining freighters (although you can if you want to). After your conversation with Jureth, all you have to do is wait until the remaining freighters exit the sector to complete the mission.

MISSION 10— ERRANT DUTY

Mission Briefing

Listen well. I have received disturbing information that I must share with you. Rendezvous with my ship at these coordinates within an asteroid field in the Uzbrin system.

Mission Overview

Objectives	Meet with Jureth.
Environment	Asteroid Field; Planet; Federation Listening Post
Basic Mission Prestige	2,000
Bonus Prestige	+100 for each Romulan destroyed
	+150 for each Romulan captured
	+150 for aiding the listening post
	-100 for refusing to aid the listening post
	-50 if the listening post is destroyed
	+300 if the Bloodlust survives
	-50 if the Bloodlust is destroyed
	-500 for disengaging and allowing both the listening post
	and the Bloodlust to be destroyed
Dialogue Prestige	To IKV Bloodlust:
	"Very well. Stand by…" (+100)
	"We are low on supplies…" (-100)

After your conversation with Jureth, set course for the Federation listening post. The Federation vessel Jureth tells you about (which is in the northwest corner of the map based on your initial position) is a diversion. Your *real* mission is to assist the *IKV Bloodlust*.

When you receive its distress call, you should be fairly close to the Romulan vessels. Proceed immediately to their position and take them out as quickly as possible. You must destroy the Romulans before they destroy the *Bloodlust*. The *Bloodlust* must survive to complete the mission. The best way to accomplish this is to concentrate your fire on the ship closest to the *Bloodlust* at all times. This tends to drive the attacker away. Once your current target has moved off, switch to the next Romulan target and repeat the process. With the *Bloodlust's* help, the mission should be over fairly quickly.

MISSION 11— AND TWO COME BARKING

Mission Briefing

After a sprint at maximum warp speed to the Kalivok-198 system, we are barely in time for our scheduled meeting with Jureth.

Mission Overview

Objectives	Hail Jureth and give your report.
Environment	Asteroid Field; Planets; Star; Klingon Listening Post
Basic Mission Prestige	3,500
Bonus Prestige	None
Dialogue Prestige	"We will begin inspection protocol..." (+25)
	"That is odd..." (+25)
	"Access the post's memory..." (-500)
	"Transporter room: beam the boarding party back..." (-100)
	"Security officer: get back..." (+250)

After Jureth chews you out for not capturing the Federation freighter in the previous mission, set course for the listening post and proceed there at warp speed. When you reach the station, follow the comm dialog tree. Shortly thereafter, Jureth's squadron appears on the scene and threatens your life. When they detect you, they head toward your position. Let them come to you. When they arrive, engage them, concentrating first on the smaller ship.

WARNING

Stars are dangerous up close. If you stray too close, expect to take heavy damage, especially if you're cloaked or otherwise unshielded. On the other hand, if you can lure the enemy into the star's corona without killing yourself in the process, you can eliminate them rather handily.

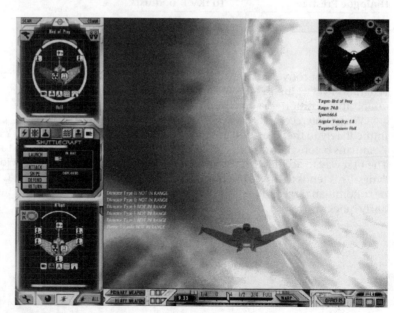

Figure 10.7 The star's corona is a very dangerous place to play.

You can take it out a lot faster, reducing the number of targets you have to deal with. Try drawing them into the star's corona (see Figure 10.7).

After you've dispatched Jureth's flunkies, order your security officer to erase the listening post's memory. Mission complete.

MISSION 12— FATHER'S DAY

Mission Briefing

"Captain, we have arrived in the Pegahl system. Our sensors are not reading any ships present."

"Do not worry. General Mi'Qogh is the definition of honor and reliability. He will be here. My father is my last hope to straighten things out."

Mission Overview

Objectives	Meet with your father to discuss recent events.
Environment	Asteroid Field; Star
Basic Mission Prestige	4,500
Bonus Prestige	None
Dialogue Prestige	None

Before you can meet with your father, you have to deal with another ambush from Jureth's squadron. There are three ships, all of them smaller than your vessel. You must destroy or capture all of these vessels before your father will appear on the scene. (You might as well destroy them since there's no bonus for capturing them.) Concentrate on one ship at a time, and make good use of your cloak, being careful not to cloak and decloak in front of any of the enemy ships (see Figure 10.8).

After you've dispatched the enemies, your father finally shows up. Complete your conversation with him to end the mission.

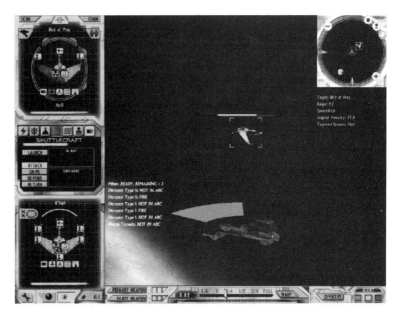

Figure 10.8 Use your cloak to throw off enemy pursuit when you're outnumbered.

MISSION 13— FRIEND OR FOE?

Mission Briefing

Greetings, son. From our recent conversation in the Pegahl system, and the data you sent in your transmission #1,458, regarding Jureth's activities of late, I can only conclude that he has either become totally consumed by a seductive scheme to grab power, or he has suffered a kind of mental breakdown. Jureth has gone into hiding, but the interrogation of some of his men has revealed that he plans to be at the inauguration ceremony for Starbase "Unity". I want you to be at that ceremony too. Find a way to talk with your brother and then report to me again on his fitness for command. I will not order the death of my own son without some form of confirmation.

NOTE

By this mission (or, hopefully, before this mission) you should have a ship of K'Tinga-class or better. The battles from here on out are quite intense, and your original K'Vort won't stand up to the punishment.

Mission Overview

Objectives	Proceed to Unity Station.
Environment	Nebula; Planets; Star
Basic Mission Prestige	4,500 (if you don't fire on Golar)
Bonus Prestige	None
Dialogue Prestige	None

Shortly after you enter the mission, you detect another Klingon vessel. This ship belongs to Golar. He's a member of Jureth's squadron, but don't fire on him! He's an ally. In fact, he needs to survive to complete the mission. Speak nicely to him.

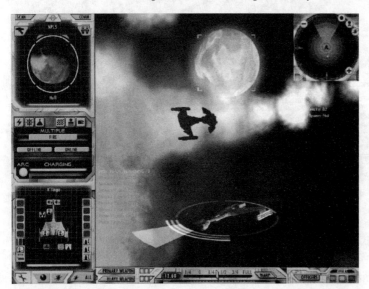

When you're in a dense nebula like the one in the "Friend or Foe?" mission, you can visually track cloaked ships against the background (see Figure 10.9). If you're observant, you can follow your enemies right up to the point when they decloak.

After your exchange with Golar, several of Jureth's ships appear on the scene. Set a course to intercept and destroy them (capture isn't an option since you can't use your transporters in a nebula). Stick close to Golar and make sure the enemies don't damage his ship too badly, and keep your eye on the star. The battle usually takes place pretty close to it.

Figure 10.9 If you keep your eyes open, you can see your cloaked enemies in a nebula.

MISSION 14—
RECALL YOUR BROTHER

Mission Briefing

Captain's Log: Jureth is to be here at the inauguration of the Unity Base—I fear the worst for my brother.

Mission Overview

Objectives	Proceed to Unity Station.
Environment	Stars; Unity Starbase
Basic Mission Prestige	2,500
Bonus Prestige	+500 for each freighter captured or disabled
	+300 for heavily damaging Jureth
	+2,000 if Golar survives
Dialogue Prestige	None

The wayward Federation freighters are your top priority. You must destroy them before they destroy Unity Starbase. After all of the initial chatter, Golar mentions the freighter. Only then can you actually fire on it. If you locate any of the freighters ahead of time, however, you can get a head start on the battle by setting course for it and getting there early. Open fire as soon as the freighters become valid targets (see Figure 10.10). Start with the one closest to the base.

After the leading freighter is taken care of, assess the fleet. If they have what's left of the freighter situation in hand, you can go after Jureth and his buddies at will. If you don't attack any of them before the last freighter is destroyed, you've missed your chance. The mission ends when the last freighter is wiped out.

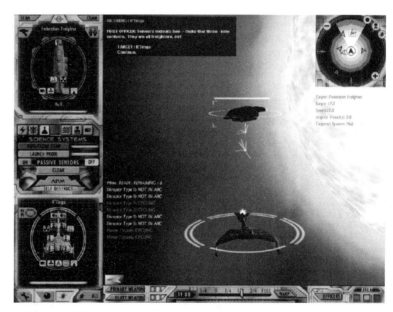

Figure 10.10 Destroy the hijacked Federation freighters before you take on Jureth and company.

MISSION 15— TO HUNT ONE'S BLOOD

Mission Briefing

Ship's Log: For my family's honor, this day I hunt my brother Jureth. My father, General Mi'Qogh, has traced Jureth to an old asteroid outpost near the Lesser Bloodstain Nebula. Despite his recent behavior, if there is any opportunity I will attempt to bring Jureth back alive, one way or another he shall answer for his crimes against the Empire.

Mission Overview

Objectives	Defeat your brother in mortal combat.
Environment	Asteroid Field; Nebula; Star; Asteroid Base
Basic Mission Prestige	5,000
Bonus Prestige	None
Dialogue Prestige	None

This one is pretty straightforward: you're out to avenge your family's honor, and Jureth has to die. He's holed up in the middle of a nebula, sticking close to an asteroid base when you first find him (see Figure 10.11).

If you cloak immediately, you can sneak up on Jureth before he powers up his engines—but that's probably not the best way to approach the battle. Since the asteroid base is equipped with the usual type-V disruptor, it's best if you can lure Jureth away from the base before the fight. You

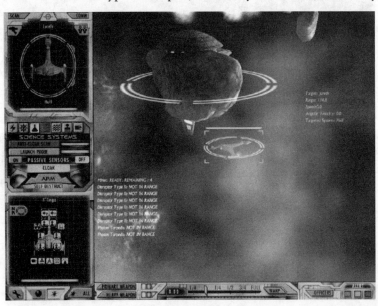

don't need to destroy the base—just Jureth.

This final battle is a tough one, and if you don't have a big enough ship, nearly impossible. One tactic you might try to strain Jureth's shields is to lure him into the dust cloud area near the star. Go in cloaked, and when you start taking damage, decloak long enough for Jureth to see you. When he moves in for the kill, recloak and head away from the star. With any luck, Jureth will tear his shields and his ship apart flying through the star's corona (see Figure 10.12) in a futile search pattern. It's a risky tactic—you could die if you're not careful—but it does work if you time things right.

Figure 10.11 Jureth is hiding out at his base—and it's best to separate him from it before you start fighting.

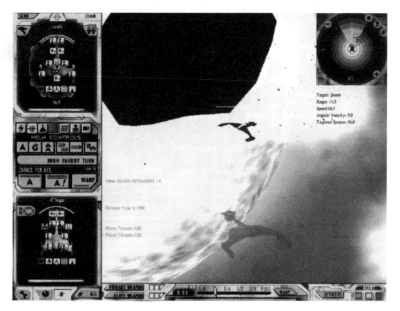

Jureth's death signals the end of the Klingon campaign. You have brought honor to the house of Mi'Qogh! *Qapla'!*

Figure 10.12 Jureth gets star-struck. Let the star do the damage as you hide and watch.

NOTE

In this last mission, you need to have the biggest ship you can get your hands on, preferably a Vor'cha or a Negh'var. Jureth is playing for keeps, and a smaller ship probably won't cut it.

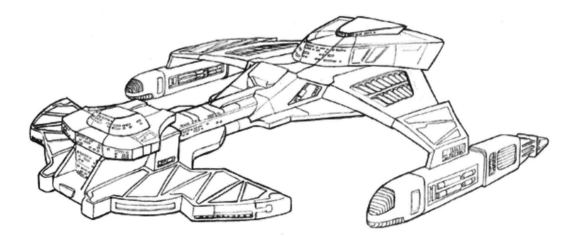

11

The Romulan Campaign

The Romulan campaign takes up where the Klingon campaign left off. Starting with a patrol mission along the Klingon-Romulan border, you take command of a starship under the supervision of the Romulan intelligence branch known as the Tal Shiar. The 17 core campaign missions set you against the other powers of the Alpha and Beta quadrants, with the ultimate goal of restoring the balance of power by destroying the starbase that the Federation and the Klingons are jointly constructing along their border.

MISSION 1—
LOOK UNDER EVERY ROCK

"We have two extremely powerful and destructive arsenals at our command. Our next actions will have serious repercussions."—Jean-Luc Picard

Mission Briefing

Military journal, supplemental: After completing a six-month security patrol of the Inner Worlds, I have been ordered to meet Admiral Arai in the Beta Ahnidea Sector near the Klingon border. Though I am happy to be doing something more interesting than scanning a steady stream of Imperial freighters for contraband, I confess to a certain trepidation at the thought of meeting with a high-ranking member of the Tal Shiar, that close to the Klingon Empire. At the Military Academy we learned that service to the Tal Shiar was a fast path to promotion…or death.

Mission Overview

Objectives	Meet with the Tal Shiar for assignment.
Environment	Asteroids; Planets
Basic Mission Prestige	750
Bonus Prestige	None
Dialogue Prestige	None

Your meeting with Admiral Arai reveals your mission: scan the Virone system for Klingon activity. It's important to note that the Admiral wants you to avoid contact with any Klingons taking action against the Klingon listening posts. If you do engage the Klingons, you lose prestige points for the mission. The longer the engagement takes, the more points you lose.

After the admiral leaves, cycle through your targets. Note that you can target three of the asteroids. One is your scanning objective. Cloak, set course for the most distant asteroid, and warp there. As you approach, a Klingon patrol ship appears and threatens you (even though you're cloaked). Respond to the hail as needed, then ignore the enemy ship. You're not here to fight. As long as you remain cloaked, it can't find you.

Move to a range of 30 or less from the asteroid and scan it. After your science officer confirms that it's the listening post you're looking for, your mission is complete. Warp out of the sector.

NOTE

Despite the fact that the campaigns form a linked narrative, you start with 100 prestige points every time you begin a new campaign. The points you earn in any previous campaigns you complete do not carry over into the next campaign.

MISSION 2— THE SOUND OF VICTORY

Mission Briefing

Military Journal 112400.6: Admiral Arai has given me the privilege of destroying the Klingon listening post I recently uncovered.

Mission Overview

Objectives	Destroy the Klingon Asteroid listening post.
	Destroy any Klingon defenders.
Environment	Asteroids; Planets
Basic Mission Prestige	750
Bonus Prestige	-750 if Admiral Arai is forced to assist
Dialogue Prestige	None

This time around, you can't target the asteroid base from your starting point, so set course to follow the directional arrow, cloak, and warp out. Eventually, you'll detect the base along your course. A Klingon patrol arrives on the scene as you approach the asteroid. Deal with the Klingon ships before you begin your attack on the base. If you have remained cloaked throughout the mission so far, you might be able to sneak up on them before they power up their engines (see Figure 11.1).

After you take care of the patrol, destroying the unarmed base is only a matter of patience. To avoid damage, stay clear of it when it explodes. You must take out both the base and the defenders to succeed.

> **NOTE**
>
> *If your hull integrity drops to 50 percent or below, Admiral Arai's Warbird arrives on the scene to assist you—and she's not too happy about it. Your prestige is reduced if the Admiral is forced to take part in the mission.*

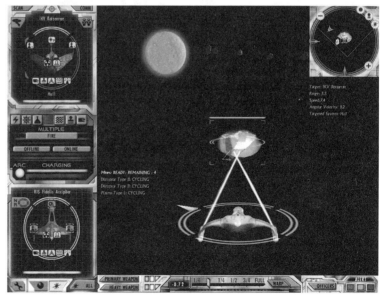

Figure 11.1 Remaining cloaked from the start might let you get in a shot before the Klingon patrol starts moving.

MISSION 3— PROFIT MOTIVE

Mission Briefing

There has been an outbreak of Tylokayd-6 on the Kesmit mining facility in the Naccar sector. As you may be aware, this virus has a 100% mortality rate, breaking the victim down into fungal slimes and mold clusters unless the patient can be treated with vaccine within 72 hours. It is imperative that this shipment of vaccine reaches Kesmit in a timely fashion. It is the only supply within range, and yours is the only available ship that can guarantee its delivery. High Command believes the Kesmit station has more than 500 citizens and forced laborers aboard. Save them all.

Mission Overview

Objectives	Escort the freighter safely to the Kesmit station.
Environment	Asteroid Field; Romulan Asteroid Base; Star
Basic Mission Prestige	1,000
Bonus Prestige	None
Dialogue Prestige	**To Romulan Ops Officer:**
	"Of course not…" (+100)

Figure 11.2 Engage the Ferengi near the base to keep the freighter safe.

Shortly after you arrive, two Ferengi Marauders appear on the scene. Target the Marauder that's doing all the talking and move in while the comm exchange proceeds (see Figure 11.2). Engaging them near the base keeps them away from the freighter and focused on you as the freighter approaches. You must keep the freighter safe. If it's destroyed, you fail the mission.

When you get the "talking" ship down to critical hull condition, the Ferengi opens a channel and tries to bribe you by giving you latinum and the vaccine. Accept the bribe by properly navigating the comm exchange to score lots of extra prestige. If you don't accept the bribe, the mission continues, but the Ferengi put a lot more effort into destroying the freighter, making your job more difficult.

You don't need to destroy the Ferengi to win. You need only to keep them busy long enough for the freighter to enter transporter range of the base. After you receive the signal that the supplies have been transferred, the mission ends successfully.

MISSION 4—DARK WATER

Mission Briefing

You are to safeguard the delivery of a shipload of dilithium crystals to the Be'Qai Military Shipyard. Do not fail. The loss of this shipment could have a profound effect upon our future fleet operations...including some initiatives that I had personally assured the Praetor would proceed on schedule.

Mission Overview

Objectives	Escort the freighters safely to the Be'Qai shipyard.
Environment	Open Space; Planet; Romulan Stardocks
Basic Mission Prestige	1,000
Bonus Prestige	+100 for each pirate captured
Dialogue Prestige	None

Enemy vessels attack the shipyard shortly after the start of the mission. As you navigate through the comm messages, select the option that orders the freighters to retreat. They must survive, and if they follow you in, they're at risk. Lock onto the closest attacker and move in for the kill.

Subcommander Lavak's ship is near one of the stardocks; try to keep it safe (see Figure 11.3). About a minute into the attack, Lavak's ship comes on line and assists you in the fight. (You also get some extra prestige if her ship survives the attack.)

Destroy all pirate vessels and keep the freighters alive to end the mission successfully.

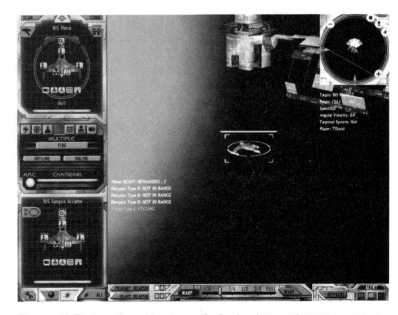

Figure 11.3 Keep Lavak's ship safe for backup and extra prestige.

MISSION 5— TIP-TOE AMONG GIANTS

Mission Briefing

This next assignment is of vital importance to not only the Empire, but to solidifying my growing faith in your prowess as a commander. The Empire requires you to investigate the old Organian Treaty Zone, in the midst of the Neutral Zone that lies between Klingon and Federation space. At this site, these two empires built a starbase called Unity One. Although the official declarations of this base's intentions from both Empires contain the usual inane references to peace and diplomacy, its position in space suggests other purposes. Deep surveillance and ship detection are likely possibilities. Not long ago, an…unforeseen…calamity befell the base, and, according to our intelligence reports, it has been brought off line.

Take this opportunity to slip into the area to gather data concerning the base and the nature of the recent disturbance. I cannot emphasize enough that extreme caution is an imperative. You must use your cloaking device and avoid all enemy contact whatsoever. If you are detected at any point, it is highly improbable that you will be able to escape. Good fortune, Commander.

Mission Overview

Objectives	Scan the Unity Station at close range.
	Maintain Cloaked Status.
Environment	Stars; Unity Starbase
Basic Mission Prestige	1,000
Bonus Prestige	None
Dialogue Prestige	None

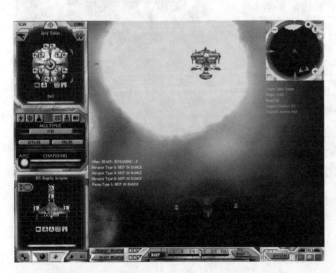

Figure 11.4 After your scan is completed. warp out of the sector immediately!

It's vital that you stick to your agenda in this mission. The sector is crawling with Federation and Klingon vessels, and you cannot win in a fight. Worse, the station has an anticloak scan, and they'll detect you after the long string of comm traffic at the start of the mission is complete.

When the mission starts, cloak immediately. Go to warp and target the Unity Starbase when it's in range. Close to within a range of 10 and initiate the scan. As soon as the scan is complete, set course for the nearest border and warp out before the entire fleet comes down on you (see Figure 11.4). If you fail to complete the scan or if you die, you fail the mission.

MISSION 6— THE ULTIMATE DUTY

Mission Briefing

I have been summoned to Kadash Prime to rendezvous with Admiral Arai at the Tal Shiar training facility. Many rumors circulate as to what goes on there…it is said that fewer than one candidate in a thousand survives, that the facility is engaged in genetic research to create the perfect defender of the Romulan Imperium, that once a candidate is accepted they disappear from all Romulan public records. Two of my friends had been inducted here. I have not heard from them since. The Tal Shiar is a doorway to mystery and adventure. Mine is a desire to rise above the political inertia of the Imperial Star Fleet. A position in the Tal Shiar would let me apply my abilities directly to the problem of defending Romulus from her enemies, without interference from the State. It is now time to enter their cloak of secrecy and see what Arai intends for me.

Mission Overview

Objectives	Complete the training exercise.
Environment	Planet; Star
Basic Mission Prestige	1,500
Bonus Prestige	None
Dialogue Prestige	None

WARNING

Although there are no dialogue prestige bonuses in this mission, there is one dialogue choice that causes the mission to end prematurely in failure. Do not respond to the rebels' pleas with this line: "I see. I was not told of such a facility. I must investigate your claims." If you respond, you lose.

This is a training mission of sorts set up by the Tal Shiar—but the consequences are real.

After you finish talking with Arai, a hijacked Romulan vessel appears near the planet. Rebels have stolen the ship and are using it to retrieve an antidote to a virus that has infected their colony. The Tal Shiar apparently planted the virus.

Move immediately to the rebel ship's position and prepare to engage. Although you *seem* to have a choice between allowing the rebels to escape and destroying them, you don't. If you allow the rebels to escape, you fail the mission. Despite the fact that it seems cold-blooded, you *must* destroy the vessel to continue the campaign (see Figure 11.5).

As soon as the ship is destroyed, Arai briefs you on the ongoing plot. Hang out until she is finished talking, and your mission is complete.

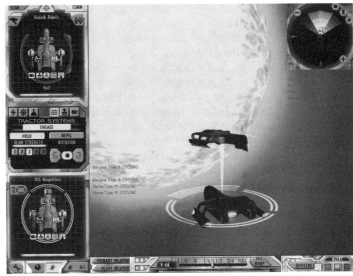

Figure 11.5 You must prevent the rebel ship from escaping to successfully complete the mission.

MISSION 7— QUIETLY I STEP

Mission Briefing

We have been sent by the Tal Shiar to a location inside Federation territory to retrieve one of our operatives from a Starfleet weapons research station.

Mission Overview

Objectives	Move across Federation territory.
Environment	Planets
Basic Mission Prestige	2,000
Bonus Prestige	None
Dialogue Prestige	None

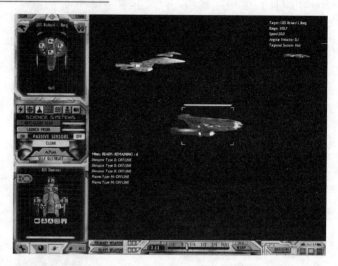

Figure 11.6 This is one Federation task force that's best left alone.

This is a dangerous situation from the moment the mission begins. You have about 10 seconds to cloak before the *huge* Federation task force detects your presence.

When you see the sheer number of ships you're up against, you'll understand that there's no way you could win in a fight (see Figure 11.6). Luckily, there's no need for you to do so. You just need to get out of the sector.

Unfortunately, you can't simply warp across the map through the Federation fleet, nor can you exit the map from any border but the one opposite your starting point. To avoid detection, turn starboard and set your course so that you pass considerably to the fleet's port flank at warp speed. Skirt the right edge of the map until you reach the far side (see Figure 11.7). If you make it across without being detected, you succeed.

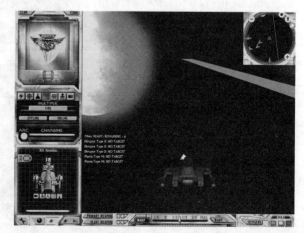

Figure 11.7 Skirt the right map border (slipping behind the far planet) to avoid detection.

MISSION 8—SNEAKERS

Mission Briefing

We have arrived in the UFC-2188 star system...the nondescript home of Starfleet Test Range "Theta". The main facility is just ahead, and alongside is the new Starfleet wonder-weapon, the *USS Incursion,* with two other ships providing perimeter security. The *Incursion* appears to be off-line and unmanned. We will begin the pickup operation with a diversionary move. By creating an explosion within the asteroid field, we will lure away the two defending ships, and can then approach the base facility and place our sensor jamming devices. Once these devices have been planted it will be relatively simple to pick up our operative from the base.

Mission Overview

Objectives	Beam an explosive device to the asteroid.
	Under cloak, travel to the base.
	Retrieve operative from base.
Environment	Asteroid Field; Federation Starbase
Basic Mission Prestige	2,500
Bonus Prestige	None
Dialogue Prestige	None

> **NOTE**
>
> *You don't have to decoy the escort starships, but there's very little chance that you'll survive a fight with them—even if you have already replaced your initial ship with a bigger one.*

Step one is to plant the decoy explosive. The only target within range is the asteroid on which you must place the device. Target the asteroid, close to within a range of 5, and beam out the explosive.

Cloak as soon as the device is deployed and warp toward the starbase. When the device is blown (you're prompted to do so via the comm; just select the only available response), the escort starships leave the starbase to investigate. Move into transporter range, dropping the jamming devices along the way (again by responding to your ops officer's comm message).

The *USS Incursion* doesn't leave, so approach the starbase from the side opposite the ship and move to a range of 5 or less (see Figure 11.8). After the Romulan operative makes contact, the operative is automatically beamed aboard. You must accomplish this fairly quickly. The jammers you dropped don't last forever.

When the operative is onboard, warp to the asteroid field and locate the shuttle that the operative tells you about. Close to weapons range and destroy it immediately. The mission ends in success when the shuttle is destroyed.

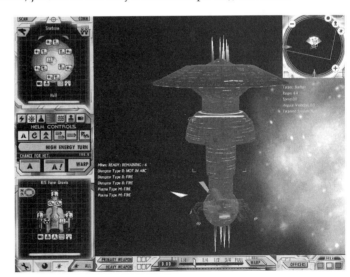

Figure 11.8 Approach the starbase from behind to prevent detection.

MISSION 9— KLINGON MARU

Mission Briefing

"Sir, we are receiving a badly distorted signal from the vicinity of RS-9012 in the Klingon Neutral Zone."

"A collapsar, is it not?"

"Yes, Subcommander. A Level-4 singularity orbiting a Type-F star. The system is marked with navigational buoys."

"Nevertheless, someone has wandered into trouble there. The message is a Klingon distress call, and the distortion is consistent with the influence of a gravitational singularity."

"Very well. In the chance that we may catch a Klingon plot unfolding, we will move into RS-9012 and see if any Klingons have survived to be interrogated. Maximum speed."

TIP

By this mission, you should have plenty of prestige to upgrade to a larger ship (if you haven't already done so). This particular mission, however, favors a small, fast vessel with a strong tractor beam— a Shrike or Hawk with at least a type-IV tractor is best. It's extremely difficult to rescue the Klingon ship unless you can move very quickly.

Mission Overview

Objectives	Rescue Klingon ship from black hole.
Environment	Star; Black Hole
Basic Mission Prestige	2,500
Bonus Prestige	50 if you don't rescue ship
Dialogue Prestige	None

Whereas in Mission 7 you (probably) had to fight your instincts and destroy your distressed target, this time around you have to do the opposite and *rescue* the beleaguered enemy. Well, you don't *have* to rescue the Klingon to accomplish the mission, but you take a huge prestige hit if you don't (see Figure 11.9).

When the mission starts, warp to about range 40 from the Klingon and start charging tractor beams. You need a powerful beam—at least strength 4. Time your approach so that you reach the Klingon just as the tractor is fully charged. When you establish a tractor beam, tow the Klingon full speed away from the black hole while carefully avoiding the gravity well yourself.

After the rescue, additional Klingons arrive on the scene. You have the choice of engaging them (in which case the rescued Klingon ship might come to your aid) or simply leaving. Leaving is preferable. You get more prestige for the mission if you avoid conflict.

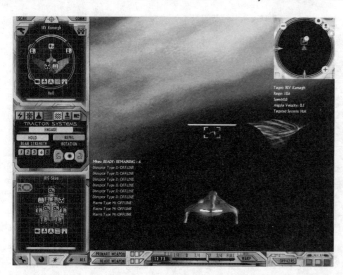

Figure 11.9 Fight your Romulan instincts and rescue the Klingon ship as quickly as possible.

MISSION 10—GRAY AREA

Mission Briefing

Greetings. Intelligence reports that the Klingons are exploiting the Hevala nebula, in the Neutral Zone. They may be attempting to hide more listening posts there. Scan the nebula carefully and report your findings. Pay particularly close attention to the asteroids.

Mission Overview

Objectives	Closely investigate all asteroids in nebula.
Environment	Nebula; Asteroid Field
Basic Mission Prestige	3,000
Bonus Prestige	None
Dialogue Prestige	None

Luckily for you, you don't really have to scan *all* the asteroids—only eight. They're marked as gray triangles on your passive sensor display. You can't detect them immediately, so move toward the cluster of asteroids directly ahead. When you see the target asteroids appearing on your passive sensors, alter course to the nearest one and scan it. You must be within range 5 to do so. Repeat this procedure with next-nearest target asteroid, and so on.

Some of the asteroids explode when you scan them (see Figure 11.10). Move away to avoid getting caught in the explosions.

After a few of the asteroids explode, a Federation freighter appears in the area. The civilian in charge banters with you, but makes no overt moves against you. Shortly thereafter, several pirate vessels enter the nebula. The freighter is no threat, but you need to clear out the pirates (in addition to scanning all of the target asteroids) to complete the mission.

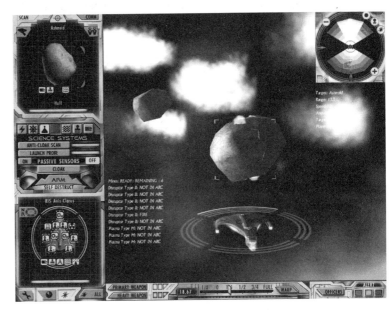

Figure 11.10 Beware the unstable asteroids!

MISSION 11—HERDING CATS

Mission Briefing

We are en route to Starbase Ja'adin for routine re-supply.

Mission Overview

Objectives	Head to Starbase Ja'adin
Environment	Asteroid Field; Planet
Basic Mission Prestige	3,000
Bonus Prestige	+300 for each freighter captured
	+75 for each freighter destroyed
Dialogue Prestige	None

When the mission begins, you're informed of a worker uprising on the planet. There are a number of rebel Romulan freighters in orbit, and your job is to take them out. Warp over to the planet (avoiding asteroids, of course). As soon as the freighters detect you, they start to run. Target the nearest freighter and engage.

After a few freighters have been captured or destroyed (after your ops officer informs you that the rebels are hardly communicating), the remaining freighters warp out of the system (if they're able to do so). This isn't a failure on your part. It simply signals the end of the mission.

MISSION 12—THE BARROWS

Mission Briefing

We are in pursuit of the rebel leader that orchestrated the impressive revolt in the Gaben Prime system. This Varus—the leader of the Reman rebels—managed to hijack our freighter convoy loading the planet's annual harvest. Though we have dealt with most of the hijacked freighters, Varus has escaped and is now headed through The Barrows—an area of "broken space" that any sane captain would avoid. Recklessness and bad terrain notwithstanding, I will corner this slave and bring him to justice.

Mission Overview

Objectives	Capture or destroy the rebel leader's ships.
Environment	Asteroid Field; Black Holes; Planet; Localized Nebulas
Basic Mission Prestige	3,000
Bonus Prestige	+500 for capturing each freighter
	+250 for destroying each freighter
Dialogue Prestige	None

The freighters are just about dead ahead of you when you begin the mission. Set course for them and catch up to them quickly. This is not a region of space you want to spend a lot of time in—or delve too deeply into if you can help it (see Figure 11.11).

All you have to do is capture or destroy the rebel freighters to complete the mission.

MISSION 13— SHINY NEW TOY

Mission Briefing

Commander, the efforts of our engineers to reverse-engineer some Federation technology have just come to fruition. Meet me at Fleet Test Facility 14, in the Gamma Virginis system.

Mission Overview

Objectives	Refit ship with new technology.
Environment	Planet; Stardock
Basic Mission Prestige	100
Bonus Prestige	None
Dialogue Prestige	None

Figure 11.11 Catch the rebel freighters before you have to chase them amidst the black holes.

TIP

The missions after this one start to get really tough. By now, you should have accumulated enough prestige to afford a large ship, preferably a Warbird. The stock version will do for now, but from this point on you should start maxing out your weapons and systems after each mission. (See Chapter 6 for suggested upgrades to Warbird-class vessels for details.)

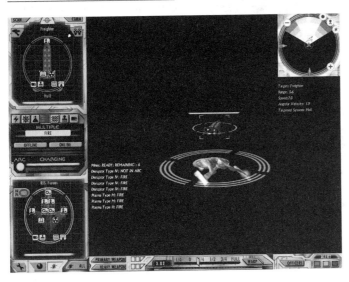

Figure 11.12 A Romulan Warbird becomes a Federation Akira courtesy of the stolen cloak/mask technology.

This is a no-fail mission (that is, unless you run into the planet and blow yourself up). You're here to have your ship outfitted with the stolen Federation cloaking system that masks your ship as a Federation vessel (see Figure 11.12).

After the cloak is installed, try it out. Fly over to the abandoned freighter and destroy it to complete the mission.

MISSION 14—YOU CAN'T MAKE ME EAT *GAGH!*

Mission Briefing

A Federation convoy has been selected as the next target to further humiliate the Alliance. The freighters should quickly fall prey to our torpedoes with the escort being the only real danger to us.

Mission Overview

Objectives	Destroy a Federation convoy posing as a Klingon raider.
	Leave no witnesses.
Environment	Open Space; Planets; Star
Basic Mission Prestige	3,500
Bonus Prestige	None
Dialogue Prestige	When the *USS MacLir* says:
	"This is unbelievable…" (+250)

Don't worry about activating your Klingon "mask." It happens automatically before the enemy detects you. Start the mission by locking onto the lead freighter (the right-most one). Move in fast and engage. Wipe out all the freighters first, ignoring the escort vessel as much as possible. (This is *much* easier to accomplish if you have a large, powerful ship, such as a Warbird.) The freighters move steadily toward the edge of the map, and you cannot let them escape (see Figure 11.13).

Afterward, turn your attention to the escort vessel and take it out. You must destroy *all* enemy vessels to succeed.

Figure 11.13 Don't let the freighters escape while you're worrying about the escort.

Chapter 11: The Romulan Campaign

MISSION 15— IN SHEEP'S CLOTHING

Mission Briefing

We continue to sow the seeds of chaos amongst our Federation and Klingon neighbors. Our next target is the Klingon military outpost at Ukhan IV. Intelligence reports indicate that no defending vessels are present. We shall take advantage of this vulnerability to strike another glorious blow against the Alliance.

Mission Overview

Objectives	Destroy a Klingon outpost posing as a Federation ship.
	Leave no witnesses.
Environment	Asteroid Field; Star; Klingon Base Station
Basic Mission Prestige	4,000
Bonus Prestige	None
Dialogue Prestige	None

You've ticked off the Federation. Now it's the Klingons' turn. Once again, you automatically transform at the start of the mission—this time, into a Federation starship. A smaller Romulan ship that is equipped with the same technology accompanies you.

The base station is your initial target, so warp in and engage. Their shields and weapons are powered down initially, so move in close and loose an alpha-strike on them before they can react (see Figure 11.14).

After a short while, a group of Klingon ships arrives. If you haven't destroyed the station, break off your attack and target the vessels. As in the previous mission, you cannot let anyone escape—and the base isn't about to go anywhere. Take out the largest ship first while your partner deals with the smaller ones.

When the reinforcements are out of the picture, finish off the base station (if necessary). Mission accomplished.

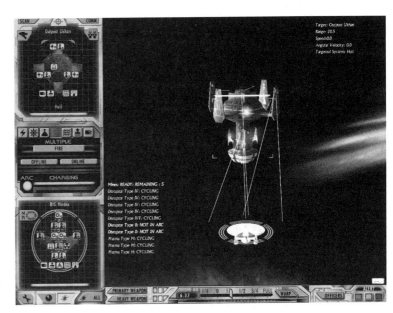

Figure 11.14 Get in your first strike before the station raises its shields.

MISSION 16— TROJAN HORSE

Mission Briefing

Our next target is a small Federation base. The ship will be disguised as a Klingon vessel bent on revenge. I will have to remember Arai's admonishment to maintain radio silence, as I fear my Klingon is as bad as ever.

Mission Overview

Objectives	Disguised as a Klingon, destroy the Federation base.
	Leave no witnesses.
Environment	Asteroid Field; Planet; Federation Battlestation
Basic Mission Prestige	4,000
Bonus Prestige	None
Dialogue Prestige	None

This mission is pretty much identical to the last—except you're disguised as a Klingon, and the target is a more heavily armed Federation battlestation. Luckily, you have two wingmen to help even the odds.

Lock onto the station and approach. As you close, the station starts sending messages to you, but they're really of no consequence. You're going to attack no matter what they say, however,

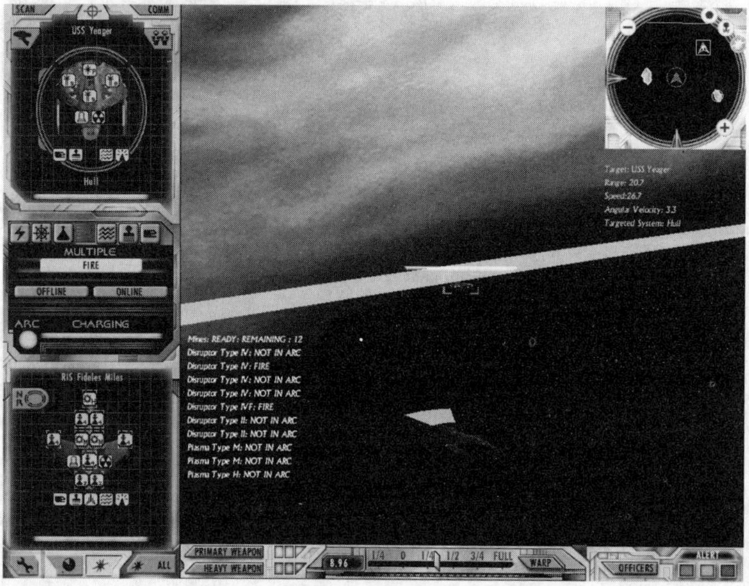

Figure 11.15 Eliminate the smaller Federation ship before it goes to warp.

move in fast. After the base's final warning to you (which comes at a range of about 20), you have only seconds before they raise their shields. Get your first shot in before that happens.

Shortly after you begin your assault on the station, the Federation reinforcements arrive in force. Once again, concentrate on the moving targets first if you haven't finished off the station when the ships appear. Moments after they arrive, the smaller Federation ship warps out. Remember: no witnesses must escape! Take out the small ship before it leaves the map (see Figure 11.15).

When the base and the reinforcements are destroyed, your mission ends in success.

MISSION 17— SALT THE GROUND

Mission Briefing

Commander, thanks in large part to your efforts we are now ready to directly assault the Unity Base. Our fleet will all be disguised as Federation warships and freighters. The freighters will be carrying hypermass detonators that will destroy not only the Unity Base, but will also crater that area of space with artificial singularities, which will permanently prevent anyone from placing a base at the location again. The freighters are the key, Commander—your mission will be to keep the freighters safe until they get close enough to release their payloads. After the base has been destroyed, help the assault force mop up what remains of the enemy fleet. We have set up pulse tachyon devices around the sector that should prevent any enemy ships from warping out to reveal what they have seen.

Mission Overview

Objectives	Destroy the Unity base.
	Protect Freighters.
	After base is destroyed, eliminate remaining resistance.
Environment	Stars; Unity Starbase
Basic Mission Prestige	4,000
Bonus Prestige	None
Dialogue Prestige	None

This is the big showdown—the culmination of Arai's plans. Your first priority is to protect the freighters. This is actually fairly easy to do, since the defending Federation and Klingon vessels tend to fire at your attack squadron rather than the innocent-looking freighters (see Figure 11.16). Get out of the way when they get near the base. They're about to do their dirty work.

It's very possible that you personally won't have to fire a shot to destroy the base—your companions and the freighters do a lot of the work for you. Just remember that, after the safety of the freighters, the base's destruction is your next-highest priority.

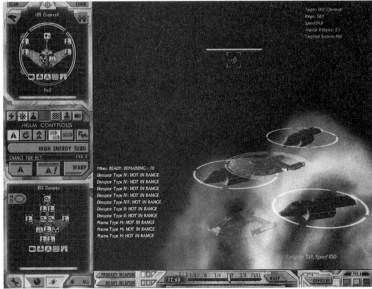

Figure 11.16 Stick with the freighters on the way in to draw fire away from them.

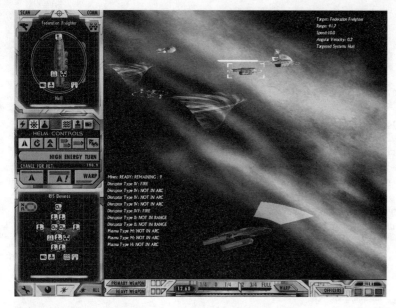

Figure 11.17 Don't let the artificial black holes swallow you when the freighters explode!

After the base is history, it's time to help your remaining wingmen mop up the rest of the enemy fleet. Remember: even though you *look* like a Federation ship, you still have a cloaking device. Use it!

Watch out for the singularities while you're in combat. You don't want to get sucked in. Actually, if the battle is raging around the former base site, you might be able to sit back and let the black holes do a lot of the work for you! (See Figure 11.18.)

When the last of the Federation and Klingon defenders are vanquished, the mission—and the Romulan campaign—end in a blaze of glory. You've brought chaos to the enemies of the Romulan Empire and won the favor of the Tal Shiar. Congratulations!

WARNING

Remember to stay well clear of the freighters when they explode. They create black holes when they go up! (See Figure 11.17.)

Figure 11.18 The enemy fleet meets its doom at the event horizon.

The Federation Campaign

You're now about to begin your final set of challenges as
a starship commander. In the wake of the destruction of
Unity Starbase, tensions are high. The Federation and
the Klingon Empire are on the verge of war after decades
of almost uninterrupted peace. Now, it's up to the forces
of the United Federation of Planets to get to the bottom
of this galactic conspiracy, and once again, bring order
and peace to the galaxy.

The Federation campaign comprises 12 core missions.
As was true in the Klingon and Romulan campaigns,
you begin your mission as a low-ranking officer with
100 prestige points. Fresh out of the academy, you
accept your first command assignment and head out
into deep space...

MISSION 1— ONE BIG, HAPPY FLEET

"The line must be drawn here. This far, no farther."—Jean-Luc Picard

Mission Briefing

This is Captain Picard. An emergency situation has arisen in the Klingon Border Region. Unity Starbase has been destroyed...apparently by renegade Klingon forces. There are reports of Klingon ships attacking both Federation military and civilian targets. I have been put in charge of investigating this matter. Your ship is in the area, so it looks like you're part of the team. Divert from your current mission and meet me at our base of operations at Starbase 297. Picard out.

Mission Overview

Objectives	Proceed to Starbase 297.
	Verify the identity of all vessels.
Environment	Open Space
Basic Mission Prestige	2,000
Bonus Prestige	None
Dialogue Prestige	None

Immediately on entering the sector, you detect the *USS Mercutio,* a Federation starship. The ship's shields are up and its weapons are armed—and yours should be, too. (Starfleet General Order 12 requires that precautions be taken if communications have not been established with an approaching vessel.) You can fire a probe when your ops officer suggests it, but it won't tell you anything you don't already know.

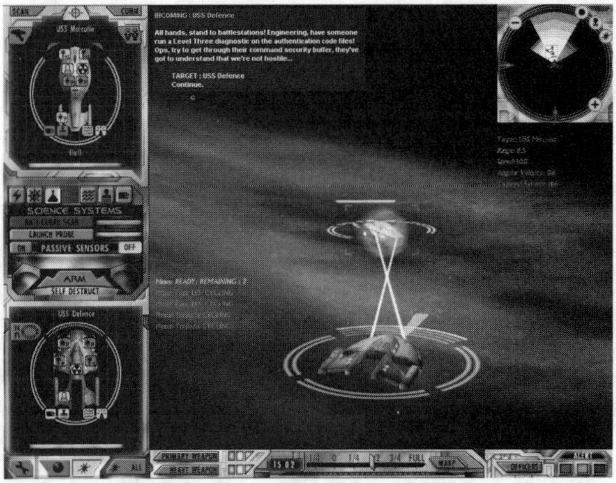

Figure 12.1 There is no way to convince the *Mercutio* you're friendly, so you might as well escalate things right away.

The *Mercutio*'s captain, as you'll discover after you eventually communicate with him, believes you're an enemy disguised as a Federation starship. Unfortunately, there's no way to convince him otherwise. You must engage the ship to succeed. You fail the mission if you leave the sector. You might as well get the first shot in (see Figure 12.1), otherwise, he'll open fire on you as soon as the communication sequence is complete and you're in weapons range.

Your ship is smaller than the *Mercutio,* and their phasers have longer range, however, the opposing ship is damaged, which helps to even the odds. When the *Mercutio*'s damage is critical, her captain signals you. Stop firing at this point. The captain is ready to listen to reason now. Mission accomplished.

MISSION 2— RENDEZVOUS AT KHITOMER

Mission Briefing

This is Starbase 297. We have plenty of reinforcements defending the starbase now, so I have new orders for you. Three Federation-registered transports have sent out distress calls from the vicinity of Khitomer IV. Rendezvous with the *USS Fuller* and investigate. Do what you can to save the freighters, then perform a Phase-I search for the *USS Minsk,* last reported in the Khitomer vicinity two days ago. I'd like to send more than two ships to Khitomer, but I'm afraid whoever is behind all this mayhem is keeping our forces stretched thin. Good luck. Picard out.

Mission Overview

Objectives	Rendezvous with the *USS Fuller.*
	Investigate the distress calls.
Environment	Open Space; Planets
Basic Mission Prestige	2,500
Bonus Prestige	None
Dialogue Prestige	None

> **TIP**
>
> *The fake freighters are slow, but they're well armed. The battle goes a lot easier if you upgrade your weapons, armor, and shields at a starbase before you start. (Better yet, upgrade to a larger ship, such as a Defiant-class light cruiser, if you can afford it.)*

The "freighters" that are sending out the distress call are on the far side of Khitomer IV. Set course for the planet and move in. The disabled Federation and Klingon ships are merely there to raise your suspicions (which should already be high at this point). You don't need to investigate them.

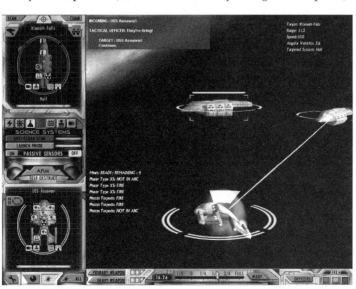

As you move in, the freighters contact you and give you a story about how they were attacked. While you listen, target one of them and continue to close. These ships are obviously not what they seem. They're Romulan ships using the "holo-cloak" technology they stole to perpetrate the destruction of Unity Starbase. (See Chapter 11 for details.) This is pretty obvious from the beginning, but you cannot fire on the freighters until they fire at you—and they do, as soon as you close to weapons range (see Figure 12.2).

Figure 12.2 Go in prepared for battle—the freighters are Romulan ships in disguise.

TIP

You can't board and activate the derelict ships, but you can target and destroy the derelicts. Do so when the enemy is on top of them and the dead ships become powerful bombs that can knock down the freighters' shields and inflict some internal damage as well.

You must destroy the enemy freighters to complete the mission. Because you're severely outgunned, you must use your superior speed and maneuverability to stay out of their forward weapons arc, delivering your attacks and dodging out of range before they can fire.

MISSION 3— WARM RECEPTION

Mission Briefing

As you may be aware, the Federation has dispatched High Commissioner Aeref Tulbarin to Krios to meet with the Klingons. Earlier this morning the starship *Columbia* was forced to leave the escort group to chase down some sensor contacts. We'll need you and your ship to take her place. If Commissioner Tulbarin's ship does not arrive safely to the conference at the Kenama Space Terminal, we lose any hope of a peaceful resolution to this crisis. If you sortie immediately for Krios at Warp 9.4, you might reach the convoy in time to provide security for the final leg of the journey. Picard out.

TIP

Before just about every Federation campaign mission, you get a chance to re-supply and refit your ship before pressing on. Take advantage of these little rest stops to optimize your ship, repair damage, and stock up on shuttles, mines, and marines.

Mission Overview

Objectives	Ensure the safe delivery of Commissioner Tulbarin to the Kenama Space Terminal.
Environment	Open Space; Planet; Klingon Starbase
Basic Mission Prestige	2,500
Bonus Prestige	None
Dialogue Prestige	None

This mission requires a ship that can deliver lots of damage quickly. If you're still commanding a destroyer, it's going to be a tough battle. A Defiant, or better, an Intrepid with at least type-X phasers makes this mission a *lot* easier. Make sure you stop at a shipyard before you accept this escort duty.

Set course for the *Amity* as soon as you arrive on the scene, and stick close to the freighter. Within moments, a Klingon ship arrives on the scene. It's a rogue, so you can deal with it as you will. Attack it as soon as you can *without* warping out to intercept it. (If you do, the Klingon warps toward the freighter, leaving you in the dust.)

The first Klingon isn't alone. Within a minute or so, the sector is crawling with renegade Klingon attackers (see Figure 12.3).

You're quite outgunned, and the Klingons are interested only in the freighter. You must stick close and take out the enemies as quickly as you can before they pound the freighter to death. To win the mission, the ambassador must be delivered safely to the base (that is, the freighter must survive) and you must eliminate all Klingon attackers.

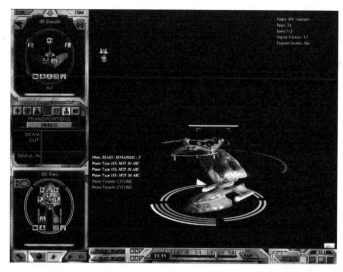

Figure 12.3 A small fleet, all intent on destroying the freighter, soon joins the first Klingon!

MISSION 4—THE STAKEOUT

Mission Briefing

This is Captain Picard. I have a new assignment for you. Starfleet and I are coming to believe that the Romulans are largely responsible for the recent trouble along the Klingon border, including the destruction of Unity One. While we prepare ourselves to sustain further attacks, you must obtain more evidence. Proceed to Earth Outpost 12 along the Neutral Zone and watch for any Romulan movement against a Federation convoy, which we have arranged to be in that area. Your job will be to ambush the attackers as they launch their attack on the convoy. You must capture or destroy at least one of the attacking vessels, and you must limit casualties to the convoy itself. We have decided not to inform the convoy of our plan at this time, in order to maximize our operational security. You will remain at Condition Green, and under silent running protocol, until you spot a force of attacking ships. We don't expect more than two Romulan ships to make an appearance, but we will be sending reinforcements just in case. Good luck. Perhaps upon your return, we will have a better idea of who and what we're dealing with.

Mission Overview

Objectives	Sit quietly, do not power up systems or go to alert.
	Once the Romulans arrive, power up and save the convoy.
	Tie up the Romulans until reinforcements arrive.
Environment	Asteroid Field; Federation Base Station
Basic Mission Prestige	2,000
Bonus Prestige	None
Dialogue Prestige	None

The Federation campaign is extremely challenging and demands constant ship refits and upgrades. Don't horde your prestige. Use it to buy better weapons and better ships at every opportunity! An Intrepid-class ship or better with as many type-X phasers as you can afford is the minimum safe vessel for this mission.

This is one mission in which you must remain at Condition Green until you spot the enemy. In fact, stay right where you are and don't move (see Figure 12.4). If you do, you'll lose before the mission even starts.

Less than a minute after the mission starts, the attack begins. Go to Red Alert, target the nearest enemy, and warp to the convoy's rescue. The convoy escort vessel engages as well to help you out.

About a minute or so into the battle, Federation reinforcements begin to arrive. As you start destroying the enemy ships, you'll notice that these "Klingons" are actually Romulan ships in disguise. (They're also less powerful than they appear, so the battle won't be as difficult as it looks initially.)

To win, at least two of the freighters must survive the attack *and* you must destroy all the attackers before they can escape.

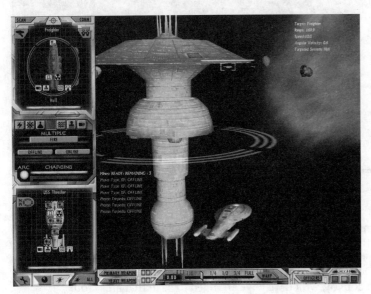

Figure 12.4 Do as the captain instructed and stay put until the enemies arrive.

MISSION 5— TERRAN: INCOGNITO

Mission Briefing

This is Captain Picard. Thanks to the Romulan debris you recovered, Starfleet has been able to determine the source of the recent unrest. The Romulans have been employing ships outfitted with stolen Incursion technology, posing as either Klingon or Federation ships, and attacking undefended outposts. We have reason to believe that the rash of "reprisal attacks" is nothing more than Romulans in disguise. We were unable to determine this earlier, as their cowardly attacks left no survivors. Now we're going to beat them at their own game. You will journey inside Romulan space to the 126 Carinae system, where Starfleet Intelligence has long suspected a Tal Shiar base to exist. Starfleet Operations needs scans of all stations and orbital installations in the system, so that the planned operations against Tal Shiar facilities can be effective. You will also need to beam down a covert Away Team into the ground facility on the planet, to appropriate some required Tal Shiar computer files.

Mission Overview

Objectives	You will be disguised as a freighter. Do not go to Red Alert.
	Scan all Romulan installations and escape undetected.
	Send away team to ground facility on planet.
Environment	Planets; Romulan Listening Posts;
	Romulan Defense Platforms; Romulan Battlestation
Basic Mission Prestige	2,500
Bonus Prestige	None
Dialogue Prestige	None

This is *not* a combat mission, and you probably wouldn't survive if it were. It's vitally important that you stick to the mission. Steering clear of all Romulan ships (you must maintain a range of 5 or more to avoid detection), start scanning the installations. The type of ship you have in this mission isn't as important as the type of computer you have. Upgrade to the best computer type your ship and budget can accommodate; type-III or better is ideal. A better computer means longer sensor range. Longer sensor range means you don't have to get as close to each facility to complete your scans.

To complete the scanning portion of the mission, you must scan all the following:

1. Comm Relay Station 251-B

2. Defense Platform A

3. Comm Relay Station 251-A

4. Battlestation

5. Defense Platform B

6. Defense Platform C

You *must* scan the targets in the order listed (follow your directional arrow and warp from target to target). You need to get them all out of the way fast. The longer you're here, the more likely it is you'll make a mistake and be detected. How close you need to be to each installation to scan it depends on your ship's computer. (The better the computer, the longer the range.) It takes several seconds to complete your scans. Do *not* use a probe! If you do, the mission ends in failure.

Patrol ships are moving around from installation to installation, but are heaviest near the comm relays. Watch their movements and approach when they're on the far side of the installation. If an enemy ship comes your way and you can't get away at impulse, go to warp and get out of range to avoid detection (see Figure 12.5).

TIP

The first comm relay is relatively clear (only one guard) at the start of the mission. Warp in before the communications chatter at the start of the mission is complete, and get the scan done before the second Romulan ship warps in several seconds later.

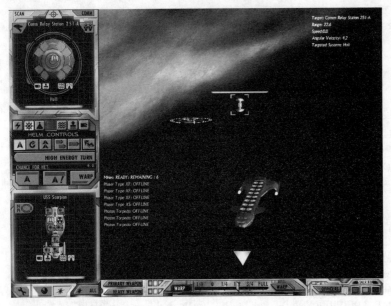

Figure 12.5 If there's no alternative, use warp jumps to avoid detection.

After the scans are complete, follow your ops officer's instructions and make your way to the planet (126 Carinae VIIA). Put the planet between you and the Romulan installations (so that you're between the planet and the sector border). Move to a range of 6 and beam down the team. Turn so that you're facing the sector border and hold position. When the alarm sounds, beam the away team up and hightail it out of the sector as fast as your warp engines will carry you.

If you accomplish all the scans without being discovered *and* beam down and retrieve the away team as instructed *and* get out of the sector safely, the mission is a success.

MISSION 6— COUNTERSTROKE

Mission Briefing

Captain, we've received a distress call from the starship *Ariel* in the C-202-Alpha system. That's the staging point for Operation "Clean Slate". If the Romulans destroy it, then we'll lose the option to attack the Tal Shiar. We'll need to move quickly.

WARNING

The ships helping you defend the freighters are very helpful—but they follow your lead to the letter. If you warp out from the battle to gain better position, they obediently follow you. If you want to prevent accidentally letting the Romulans take out your freighters, make sure you don't accidentally lead your wingmen away!

Mission Overview

Objectives	Rescue vessels under Romulan attack.
Environment	Open Space
Basic Mission Prestige	2,000
Bonus Prestige	None
Dialogue Prestige	None

You arrive on the scene to find the Federation convoy under Romulan attack. Warp in immediately with your wingmen and engage. Concentrate on a small ship first. You can take it out fast and reduce the number of targets (see Figure 12.6).

If the battle rages long enough, additional Federation reinforcements start arriving on the scene at staggered intervals to make the remaining battle a bit easier for you.

Destroy all the Romulan attackers before they destroy more than two members of the convoy to win the mission.

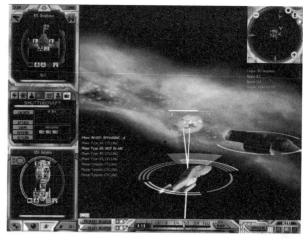

Figure 12.6 Reduce the number of enemy targets quickly by first destroying a small vessel.

MISSION 7— FORCED ENTRY

Mission Briefing

We have been cleared to initiate Operation "Clean Slate" against the Tal Shiar. The Enterprise will lead Task Force Nine in this endeavor. We will try to restrict our focus to the Tal Shiar, but the Romulans will undoubtedly not take kindly our presence within their borders. Mission data upload will commence at 0800 hours. Our first target will be the Romulan outpost R-56, in the Aegand system. We will neutralize it and open a path for our ships to come and go as they please while we complete our mission. We will undoubtedly face heavy resistance from Romulan forces, but I have confidence our forces will prevail. Godspeed. Picard out.

Mission Overview

Objectives	Capture or destroy the Romulan outpost.
	Destroy or capture all remaining Romulan ships.
Environment	Open Space; Romulan Battlestation
Basic Mission Prestige	1,500
Bonus Prestige	None
Dialogue Prestige	None

Although your primary mission is to destroy the battlestation, concentrate on the defending vessels first. The station isn't going anywhere, and it's a lot easier to assault the base after the defenders are neutralized. While you're taking care of the Romulan ships, try to stay out of range of the base's powerful weapons.

After all the defenders are neutralized, move in along with the rest of the fleet and destroy the base. Make sure you're a good distance away when it blows.

Mission accomplished!

MISSION 8—
OPERATION ROUNDUP

Mission Briefing

Greetings Captain. The scout ship *USS Lovell* has detected a force of Romulan infiltrator ships in the Utanya system. Your task force will proceed to Utanya and ambush these vessels. The *Lovell* is currently monitoring the fleet, so make your best speed to arrive before she's detected. Destroy as many Romulan ships as you can. The Klingon Empire has requested that their ships be allowed to accompany us on this mission, and Starfleet has obliged. We have the potential to deal the Romulans a decisive blow here, Captain. Good luck. Picard out.

TIP

Have you been keeping up with your ship upgrades? You definitely want to be beyond the light-cruiser stage by the time you take on this mission. Nothing short of a Nebula-class vessel has much chance of survival. Fast weapons are a must, as well. Type-XF or XIF phasers are ideal if you can afford the upgrade.

Mission Overview

Objectives	Ambush and destroy a Romulan infiltration force.
Environment	Open Space
Basic Mission Prestige	1,500
Bonus Prestige	None
Dialogue Prestige	None

The Romulans are using their holo-cloaks to disguise their ships as Klingon vessels. Don't worry about targeting the wrong ships, though. Use your passive sensors and point yourself toward the red targets. The Romulan vessel names are correct in your target reticule information display, and you can tell the difference between the ships easily enough by watching the weapons they fire—and whether they fire them at you and the other Federation ships.

The Romulan ships aren't as small and helpless as their Klingon images make them appear. Enter the fray cautiously and isolate the vessels from one another if possible before you engage. A full-on assault from multiple ships can take out even a powerful vessel (see Figure 12.7).

The battle is fierce but relatively brief. You and your taskforce should be able to make quick work of the enemy. When the Romulans are down to two ships, they drop their holo-cloaks and warp for the sector edge. Do your best to catch and destroy them, but don't sweat it if they get away. The mission is complete whether the Romulan vessels are captured, destroyed, or forced to retreat.

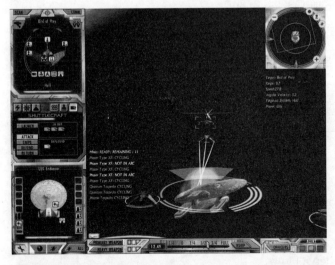

Figure 12.7 You'll pay dearly for rushing headlong into battle against multiple enemies.

MISSION 9— ELUSIVE QUARRY

Mission Briefing

This is Captain Picard…take charge of Task Group 15 and launch an immediate attack on Admiral Arai's Tal Shiar headquarters at 126 Carinae. Neutralize all resistance. The fleet is to regroup at Location Gray at the conclusion of your mission.

Mission Overview

Objectives	Lead the attack against Admiral Arai's headquarters at 126 Carinae.
Environment	Planets; Romulan Listening Posts;
	Romulan Defense Platforms; Romulan Base Station
Basic Mission Prestige	5,000
Bonus Prestige	None
Dialogue Prestige	None

Go to Red Alert immediately and start fighting, starting with the defending vessels. Try to stay out of range of the station and defense platform weapons.

A minute or so after the assault begins, the *Enterprise* arrives in the sector—or so it would seem. Despite the fact that the incoming message *seems* as if it's coming from Picard, it's really Admiral Arai, and the *"Enterprise"* is her holo-cloaked Warbird. Don't fall for it. During the comm exchange, ask the ship to transmit its security code. When "Picard" refuses, *you* refuse to lower your shields. At this point, Arai drops her holo-cloak and the battle can begin.

Break off immediately and deal with Arai (see Figure 12.8). Stay behind the ship if possible. A Warbird can tear you apart if you're in its forward weapons arc. When she is sufficiently damaged, she'll taunt you then turn tail and run. Let her go. You can't destroy her.

After Arai leaves, concentrate your efforts on the remaining Romulan ships. When they're neutralized, knock out the defense platforms between you and the base to weed out the resistance and then, finally, blast the station into oblivion.

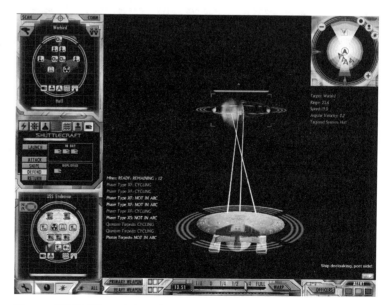

Figure 12.8 When Admiral Arai reveals herself, show her that nobody gets away with impersonating Jean-Luc Picard!

MISSION 10—A LIGHTLY SCORCHED EMPIRE

Mission Briefing

We now focus our efforts upon the Gamma Virginis system, one of the few systems that Earth was forced to leave in Romulan hands at the conclusion of the Earth-Romulan War in 2160. Intelligence indicates that the Tal Shiar is deploying the holo-cloak units aboard its starships at the shipyard here. We must neutralize its ability to deploy these devices of deception.

The risky portion of the mission we are assigning to you, since you have developed a certain proficiency at special operations. You will need to send an away team aboard the shipyard, so that we may acquire the database of all Romulan ships that have received the holo-cloak upgrade…and can begin tracking them.

Mission Overview

Objectives	Send team to space dock to acquire plans.
	Destroy Romulan shipyard.
Environment	Planets; Romulan Battlestation; Romulan Space Docks
Basic Mission Prestige	5,000
Bonus Prestige	None
Dialogue Prestige	None

Figure 12.9 After retrieving the away team, hightail it away from the space docks and battlestation to join the other ships in battle.

Let the other ships handle the battle at first. Your first priority is to deliver the away team to a space dock. Set course for one of the space docks and warp there immediately. Both space docks are in close proximity to the battlestation, so make sure that the shield you're dropping to transport the away team is facing *away* from the battlestation. Reinforce the shield facing the station. The away team takes only a few seconds to complete their mission, but you could take some heavy fire during that time. After the away team is done, beam them back and warp out of the battlestation's weapons range (see Figure 12.9).

Although you might be tempted to wipe out the space docks right away, take out the defending ships first. If you blow up a space dock while defenders are still in the area, the defending vessels self-destruct and turn into black holes, making the sector extremely dangerous.

Once the defenders are destroyed, it's time to complete your second objective. If you destroy the battlestation first (which should be a relatively easy task if most of your attack force is still intact), you can take out the space docks at your leisure.

MISSION 11— THE LUDDITE SYNDROME

Mission Briefing

We're about to depart for Miaplacidus, so I will keep this short. As Task Force Nine enters the Miaplacidus system, your ship will lead the group assigned to eliminate planetary defenses and insert an away team equipped with detpacks into the Voran City factory complex on the northern continent. The coordinates have been transmitted to your ship's computer. There are not expected to be any civilians present at the time, as the Romulans are observing a cultural holiday. The assault will be confined to the holo-cloak module replication units. Good luck. The fleet will be moving out at 0300 hours.

Mission Overview

Objectives	Eliminate the Romulan resistance.
	Destroy replication facilities on planet.
Environment	Open Space; Planet; Romulan Battlestation; Romulan Defense Platforms.
Basic Mission Prestige	2,100
Bonus Prestige	None
Dialogue Prestige	None

To complete the away-team mission, you must take out all the planetary defenses—that means the battlestation and all the defense platforms. The easiest way to handle this is, as always, to handle the moving targets first. Once all the Romulan ships are off your tail, the stationary facilities are a lot easier to deal with (see Figure 12.10).

When the situation is under control, turn your attention to the planet. If the planetary defenses are gone, when you close to within range 10, you get a communication that tells you the away team is ready to beam down.

Figure 12.10 The base and defense platforms are sitting ducks after the Romulan fleet is out of the way.

Blast a hole in the planet's shields, close to a range of 5, and beam down the away team. When they signal their mission is complete, beam them back.

When the away team has completed its mission and all Romulan ships and facilities are destroyed, your job here is done.

MISSION 12— THE POINT OF NO RETURN

Mission Briefing

We are ready to proceed with what we hope will be the final part of this campaign. We have traced Admiral Arai on long-range sensors to the Romii system, where Starfleet Intelligence believes there to be the main headquarters of the Tal Shiar. The Federation Council, based partly upon our recommendations, has mandated the removal of Admiral Arai as a precondition for normalizing our relations with the Romulans. The Romulans, as we might have expected, have yet to respond to this demand. In the absence of any cooperation from the Romulans on this point, Task Force Nine is to proceed to Romii immediately. You will lead the operation to seize Arai and destroy the Tal Shiar headquarters facility. It will be necessary to deal with the planetary defenses before you can safely perform your mission, but hopefully the fleet we have assembled for this operation will be adequate against whatever the Romulans can throw at us.

Mission Overview

Objectives	Eliminate orbital stations.
	Capture Admiral Arai.
	Neutralize Tal Shiar headquarters.
Environment	Open Space; Romulan Battlestation; Romulan Defense Platforms
Basic Mission Prestige	2,100
Bonus Prestige	None
Dialogue Prestige	None

By now, you should know the standard drill in base assault-type missions: take out the moving targets first. Immediately locate and engage the Romulan defense fleet before you even think about the orbital facilities (see Figure 12.11). Make the large ships your top priority. If you take them out early, the smaller ships in your attack group have a better chance of surviving the initial phase of the mission.

After you dispatch the enemy ships, join the *Enterprise* back at the orbital facilities. By this time, Picard has probably taken out a lot of the planetary defenses for you. Pitch in and help finish off the defense installations.

When Picard signals you to beam down the assault teams, move to within range 5 of the planet, and take care of the away team missions as instructed by the comm messages. After team Bravo has accomplished its mission and

TIP

You really need a Sovereign-class ship for the final mission, so if you don't have one already, now is the time to buy one. You should also upgrade the ship's weapons (replacing the existing forward and 360-degree phasers with type-XIF is very helpful), and stock up on shuttles and mines for the final fight.

you have beamed everyone back on board, move away from the planet and join the rest of the Federation fleet. Within moments, Romulan reinforcements arrive. Prepare for one of the most intense battles in your Starfleet career (see Figure 12.12).

There will be a lot of casualties in this battle—but as long as you aren't one of them, you needn't mourn overly long. After the last of the Romulan ships is destroyed, the mission ends in a rousing success.

Congratulations, captain. Thanks to you, order has been once again been restored to the galaxy. Well done!

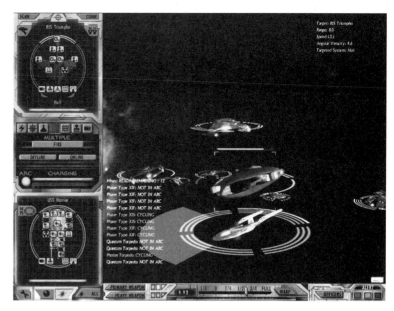

Figure 12.11 Join the other ships in your taskforce and engage the Romulan vessels.

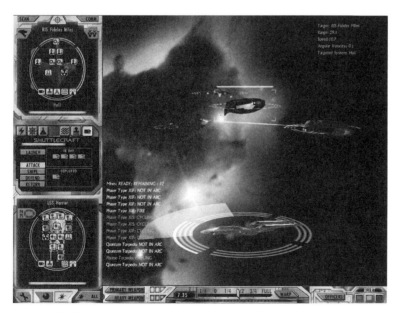

Figure 12.12 The Romulan reinforcement fleet is full of Warbirds and other large ships.

13

General Campaign Missions and Conquest Campaigns

Commanding a starship isn't a constant series of epic battles that shake your empire to its very roots or alter the course of life in the universe. Many of the missions available to you are more routine.

The primary focus of every campaign in *Starfleet Command III* is the main campaign's progression—the missions described in Chapters 10–12. You do, however, have some downtime between the core missions, and during that time, there are a number of missions you can undertake. You aren't *required* to participate in these missions, but their successful completion helps you gain experience and earn extra prestige for promotions, ship upgrades, and purchasing new starships.

General campaign missions come in six basic varieties, and you can find them by exploring the map and checking for missions in each sector (see Chapter 9 for details). The amount of prestige you gain for successfully completing general campaign missions varies by mission type. You can also *lose* prestige points if you fail to complete the mission, but you lose prestige in non-core campaign missions only if you die. If you disengage from the mission with your ship intact (even if it's full of holes), your prestige for the mission is zero.

The following sections describe the conditions and strategies for every general campaign mission type available in the game. The final section of the chapter describes the "conquest" campaign, of which these missions are also a part.

BASE ASSAULT

> *"Twenty particles of space dust per cubic meter, 52 ultraviolet radiation spikes, and a class-two comet. Well, this is certainly worthy of our attention."*—Jean-Luc Picard

Mission Briefing

You've entered enemy territory. Neutralize the enemy base at all costs.

Mission Overview

Objectives	Destroy the enemy base plus all defenders and auxiliary facilities.
Typical Enemies	Enemy base; defense platforms; 1–3 enemy ships
Basic Mission Prestige	750

A Base Assault is *not* a mission you should take on lightly. If you've played through any of the three main campaigns, you've seen what kind of firepower an enemy base can muster. It's a difficult mission to undertake even when you have a large assault force as backup. To take it on alone is tantamount to suicide. If you *must* test your prowess in a base assault, make sure you wait until late in the campaign, when you have a powerful starship. Meandering into this mission with a frigate or a light cruiser is just plain silly—a waste of time and prestige (see Figure 13.1).

The strategy when assaulting a base of your own free will is the same one that you use when you're forced to assault a base in the course of the core campaign. Take out the moving targets (the defending ships) first, staying clear of the base and defense platforms in the process if possible. Then, move in and take out the stationary targets. You don't have the benefit of a friendly armada in the sector, so launch some shuttles to give the enemy something to shoot at besides you. If you need some base assault practice, you might want to try your hand at the Base Assault skirmish mission a few times before you attempt this task in a campaign.

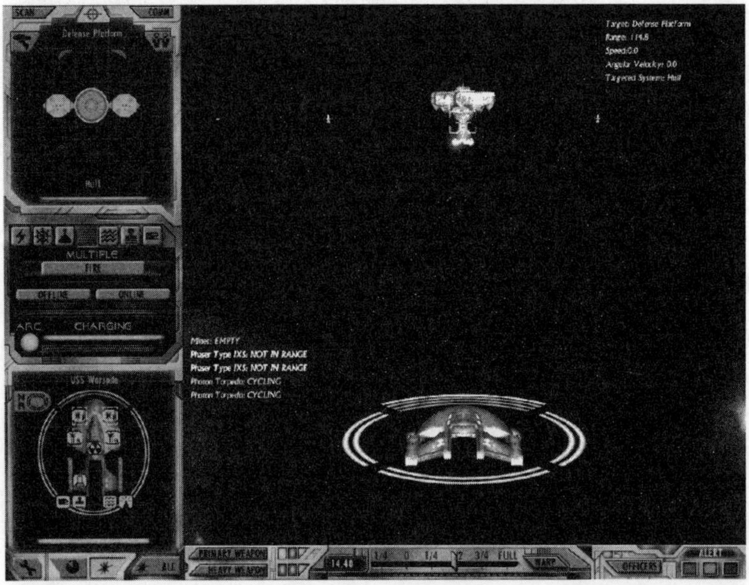

To succeed, you must capture or destroy all enemy targets in the sector. There are easier ways to rack up prestige, so unless you're tremendously confident in your abilities and in your ship, avoid base assault missions such as the Phyrox Plague.

Base assaults always take place in enemy territory.

Figure 13.1 Preparing to attack a starbase with a destroyer. You might as well just activate the self-destruct.

CONVOY ASSAULT

Mission Briefing

You have a chance to strike an economic blow against the enemy.
Intercept and destroy as many freighters as you can, then disengage.

Mission Overview

Objectives	Destroy as many freighters as possible.
Typical Enemies	Freighters (6)
Basic Mission Prestige	100 per freighter
Bonus Prestige	100 if all 6 freighters are destroyed

It doesn't get any easier than a convoy assault.
The enemy convoy, which usually consists of six
freighters, is almost always unprotected. That
means minimal resistance and lots of slow, lumbering targets (see Figure 13.2). You can accomplish a
Convoy Assault mission regardless of the type of
ship you're commanding—they're that easy.

The enemy freighters start off on a direct course
for the edge of the map, and they don't tend to
deviate widely from their initial track for any reason. The only trick here is to destroy the freighters
before they can disengage. Start
with the lead ship (the one closest
to the map edge) and work your
way back.

To succeed, you must destroy
at least half of the enemy
freighters. Anything less is
deemed a failure and you don't
gain any prestige.

Convoy assaults usually occur
in neutral or enemy territory.

NOTE

*If you disengage before you complete the
mission, or if some of the freighters get away,
and the convoy is still in the sector when you
return to the Mission screen, you can restart the convoy assault mission (with the enemy ship condition and
number unchanged from the time you disengaged) to take
care of the remaining freighters.*

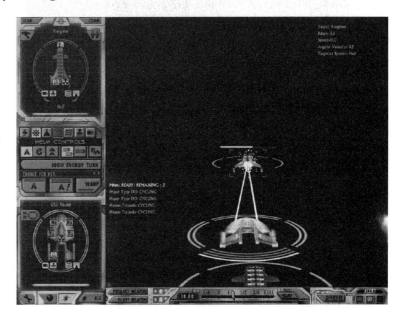

Figure 13.2 Convoy assaults are an easy way to pick up some
extra prestige.

DISTRESS CALL

Mission Briefing

You've received a distress call from a nearby ship. You're currently heading to their location.

Mission Overview

Objectives	Destroy the attacking ships before they destroy the friendly freighter.
Typical Enemies	1–3 attackers (see description for details)
Basic Mission Prestige	100

In a Distress Call mission, you are called on to rescue a friendly freighter that is under attack by enemy forces. There are always 1–3 enemies present. The origin of the enemy ships is usually based on the empire you're currently playing as. The most likely attackers for each empire are shown in Table 13.1 (though other races might be involved in the attack depending on the circumstances).

Your Empire	Attackers
Klingons	Rakelli
Romulans	Pirates
Federation	Ferengi
Borg	Ferengi

Table 13.1 Most Likely Attackers in a Distress Call Mission

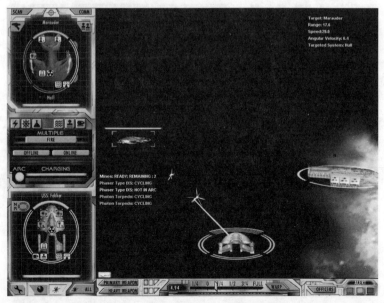

Figure 13.3 Engage the enemy as soon as you can to prevent damage to the freighter.

In this scenario, you can expect a little help from the freighter, but the bulk of the responsibility is yours. Target the enemy closest to the freighter and warp in to engage (see Figure 13.3). The enemy ships target the freighter almost exclusively.

The mission is pretty straightforward. If you destroy all of the attackers before they destroy the freighter, you succeed. If not, you fail. You don't have any backup in a Distress Call mission, so if you need a little extra firepower, launch your shuttles. They come in handy, especially after you get the enemies' shields down.

Distress Call missions can occur anywhere, but are most common in friendly sectors.

PATROL

Mission Briefing

Your mission is to engage any enemy ships. If you're heavily outnumbered, disengage. Survival is its own reward.

Mission Overview

Objectives	Destroy the attacking vessel(s).
Typical Enemies	Varies
Basic Mission Prestige	At least 100, but varies according to difficulty.

A Patrol mission is a basic skirmish with one or more enemy starships. Your goal here is simply to destroy your target(s) before they destroy you. If you are outnumbered or outgunned, you can disengage without facing any penalties—and you should do so! It's better to run away than to severely damage or lose your ship in a hopeless fight.

If you disengage from combat before you defeat the enemy, you can re-engage the enemy target while it's in the same sector by clicking Missions and attacking the same target from the Mission Selection screen. When you re-engage, the target vessel is in the same condition it was in when you disengaged unless there is an enemy base in the sector (in which case the enemy might be repaired). Your ship's condition is the same as before you disengaged, too (unless there is a *friendly* base in the sector and you repair it), so think twice before re-engaging a target when your ship is severely damaged.

Patrol missions usually take place in enemy or neutral space.

Attacked!

When you enter a sector where an enemy ship is on patrol (or an enemy ship enters the sector you're in), you might be attacked by that ship (see Figure 13.4). This mission is identical to a Patrol mission except that, if you refuse the mission, you lose all of your prestige and might lose your current ship as well (you are given a ship equal to the one with which you started the campaign).

Even if you don't want to fight, accept an Attacked mission to avoid that consequence. If you enter the mission then immediately retreat off the map, the fight is considered a draw and you are not penalized.

This mission is most likely to occur when you are in enemy or neutral territory.

Figure 13.4 When an enemy ship attacks you, accept the challenge or suffer severe penalties.

PLANETARY ASSAULT

Mission Briefing

Attack and destroy all orbital planetary defenses. This will provide an effective embargo of the planet, cutting it off from off-world assistance.

Mission Overview

Objectives	Destroy all orbital facilities and defending ships.
Typical Enemies	Defense platforms; 1–4 enemy ships
Basic Mission Prestige	1,500

Handle Planetary Assault missions in the same way you handle Base Assaults. Make the defending ships your top priority. Warp in, target a ship, and lure it out away from the defense platforms. Even the most powerful starship gets torn up when taking fire from multiple defense platforms and several ships simultaneously (see Figure 13.5). Launch some shuttlecraft so that your enemies have other targets to fire at besides you.

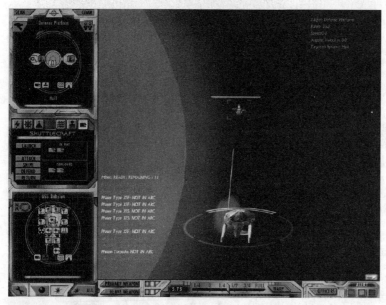

After the defending ships are out of the picture, take out the defense platforms one at a time, setting your course so that you're in range of only one platform at any given time. The mission is a success when you've eliminated all defense platforms and defending ships.

Planetary assaults always take place in enemy territory.

Like Base Assaults, Planetary Assaults are not easy missions. You should avoid them until you have a very large, very well-armed starship. Don't even consider this mission early in the campaign.

Figure 13.5 The Sovereign-class starship's tattered shields show why you should lure the defending ships away from the defense platforms in a Planetary Assault mission.

Chapter 13: General Campaign Missions and Conquest Campaigns

SCAN

Mission Briefing

You are to scan the planet in this sector and retreat. You may defend yourself if attacked. To complete the scan, get to within a distance of 10 and scan with your deep scanners.

Mission Overview

Objectives	Scan the planet.
Typical Enemies	Possibly 1–2 (see the following)
Basic Mission Prestige	50

Scan missions, which usually occur in friendly territory, are generally quite simple. When the mission begins, warp to the target planet, close to within the specified range, and scan it. When you're notified that the scan is complete (typically around 10 seconds or so), the mission ends successfully.

There is about a 50 percent chance that 1–2 enemy ships could be in the area. If they're present, you must destroy them in addition to scanning the planet to complete the mission. The type of enemy present (if any) varies from mission to mission, but largely depends on which empire you're playing as. (See Table 13.1 earlier in this chapter for details.)

Since they are the easiest noncritical campaign missions, Scan missions aren't worth a lot of prestige. They are, however, very common and very easy. If you accept every Scan mission that comes along, 50 prestige points per mission adds up quickly.

SHIPYARD ASSAULT

Mission Briefing

You've entered enemy territory. Destroy the enemy shipyard at all costs.

Mission Overview

Objectives	Destroy all enemy space docks and defending ships.
Typical Enemies	6 space docks; possibly 1 or more enemy starships
Basic Mission Prestige	100 per space dock
Bonus Prestige	100 if all six space docks are destroyed

Shipyard Assaults offer the best prestige for effort ratio of any general campaign mission type (see Figure 13.6). Space docks are completely defenseless and they don't move—how's that for an easy target? To top it off, there are seldom any enemy ships present to defend the space docks, so the only way you can get hurt in this mission is to be too close to one of them when they explode. (Large facilities pack quite a wallop when they blow.) In fact, the space docks are usually close enough to one another so that when one explodes, the nearby space docks take moderate damage.

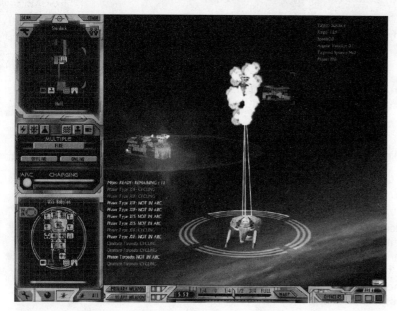

Figure 13.6 If you thought assaulting a freighter convoy was like shooting tribbles in a barrel, wait until you take on a bunch of defenseless space docks!

If there are any enemy ships in the area, deal with them first. Otherwise, just take an enjoyable impulse romp through the sector and wipe out all six space docks at your leisure. When enemy targets are destroyed, the mission is complete. If for some reason you leave before you destroy all of the targets and have to come back later to finish them off, the ones you've destroyed are still destroyed when you return.

Shipyard Assault missions always occur in enemy territory in sectors that contain an enemy base or planet. Since resistance is minimal, you don't need a huge, powerful starship to accomplish this mission.

CONQUEST CAMPAIGNS

Each of the three major empires actually has two campaign types available. The main story campaign for each follows the progression described in Chapters 10–12. The other type of campaign, Conquest, is quite different.

Instead of following a storyline with a set number of missions, Conquest campaigns are completely freeform. Your goal is to conquer the entire galaxy. You do this by destroying all enemy units and facilities on the entire galactic map. Basically, Conquest campaigns consist of a string of general campaign missions (as described in this chapter). You move from sector to sector, taking on the missions of your choice and gaining prestige with the goal of being the sole survivor. If you follow the strategies presented throughout this chapter, you should be galactic emperor in no time.

NOTE

Although the Borg don't have a Story campaign like the other empires, they do have a Conquest campaign. Galactic conquest is certainly an appropriate goal for the Collective.

14

Skirmish Missions

in both single- and multiplayer modes. These missions are one-off adventures that are great for practicing against the AI to hone your command skills or as quick online encounters to test your mettle against friends and strangers all over the world. To make things even more interesting, you can play any of the four skirmish mission types in a variety of deep space conditions ranging from open space to dense asteroid fields and nebulae.

All combat basics apply, so brush up on the tips and tricks in Chapter 3. Skirmish missions also have their own rules, however, and multiplayer adds a whole new dimension to *SFC3* combat.

This chapter walks you through the rules of engagement for each mission type and provides some tips and strategies on how to excel against both AI and human opponents.

BASE ASSAULT

Rules and Objectives

Teams:	2
Team 1:	Attackers
Team 2:	Defenders
Ship Selection/Customization Allowed?	Yes
Attacker Objectives:	Primary objective is to destroy the starbase.
Defender Objectives:	Primary objective is to neutralize all attacks on the starbase.
End Conditions:	The mission ends when the starbase is destroyed or when all attackers are neutralized.

The Base Assault mission pits two teams against each other, with one team attacking and one team defending a starbase. The starbase type depends on the empire defending it. If multiple empires are defending the base, the origin of the base is decided at random from among the defending races.

The number of attackers and defenders depends on the number of players (AI or human) on each team. The mission can be reasonably easy or extremely difficult depending on the ships selected and the modifications made to each. To level the playing field (especially in a multiplayer game) set a reasonable point limit on ships. That way, you won't end up taking on a fleet of Warbirds and a starbase at the same time.

That said, you should select the best ship you can within the specified point limits. Take some time to refit your ship with the heaviest shields and weapons it can handle without turning it into an underpowered, slow-moving barge. Starbases dish out a lot of damage, and it takes a lot of damage in turn to blast through their shields.

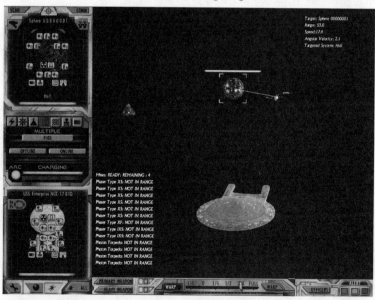

When you're on the attacking team (Team 1), your goal is to destroy the base. As is true in campaign missions that require you to assault a base or other stationary target, concentrate on taking out the defending ships first. Try to lure the defenders as far from the base as possible so that you can deal with them without taking damage from the base's weapons at the same time. After all the defenders are out of the way, you can move in and deal with the base itself. If you have other ships on your team, have some of the ships engage the defenders while the rest begin the base assault (see Figure 14.1).

Figure 14.1 Divide and conquer: Assign some attackers to keep the defending ships busy while the rest warp in to attack the base.

When you're defending the base, avoid falling for the same trick. If you succumb to the temptation to meet the attackers far from the base, you not only risk allowing some of the attack force to slip past while you're otherwise occupied, you also forego the extra firepower provided by the base's defenses. If you lure the attackers into a close-in engagement, the base weapons can be of great assistance in eliminating the enemy vessels.

BATTLEFEST

Rules and Objectives

Teams:	Up to 6
Ship Selection/Customization Allowed?	No
Mission Description:	Players begin with control of a frigate. As ships are destroyed, they're replaced with progressively more powerful ships. After a player's last ship is destroyed, the player is eliminated.
End Conditions:	Last team/player standing wins.

Battlefest skirmishes are excellent scenarios in which to test your raw starship command skills. Because you're unable to select and customize your starship in these missions, you cannot rely on custom configurations or ship-specific tricks to get you through. You must find a way to prevail with the ships you're given.

The ship progression in a Battlefest skirmish is as follows:

1. Frigate

2. Heavy Cruiser

3. Dreadnought (Battlecruiser)

A Battlefest is a war of attrition. The key to victory is holding on to each of your ships as long as possible while doing as much damage and eliminating as many enemy ships as possible. The longer you can keep from jumping up to your next-strongest ship, the better off you are.

Just because everyone starts with the same ship class, don't assume that you're all equally matched. If you're out of sensor range when you begin, use a probe to determine the enemy's ship type and loadout. Browse through Chapters 4–7 to familiarize yourself with each ship type, and plan your attack and defense accordingly.

If you're successful in the initial match-up, you find yourself up against a larger, better-armed enemy ship. Even so, you can survive for a long time if you play to your strengths. Use your smaller ship's maneuverability and speed to stay out of your opponent's most formidable weapon arcs (see Figure 14.2). Concentrate your fire on a single shield when possible. Even if you can't destroy your target, try to soften it up as much as possible so that, when you get your next-strongest ship, the enemy is an easier target because of its weakened state.

When you change ships, there is a brief targeting blackout period—the enemy can't target you and vice-versa. Take this time to orient your ship on the enemy's last known position (look for the debris cloud from your last ship's explosion), and start moving in that direction. As soon as your weapons are charged and you can target the enemy, begin your assault anew.

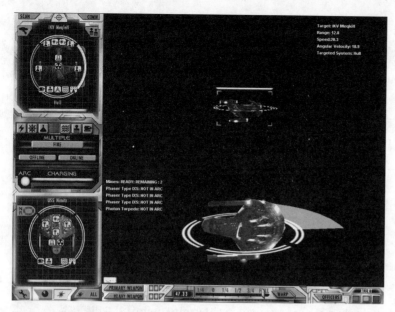

Figure 14.2 Take advantage of your ship's performance to survive against larger vessels.

Your strategy must change when there are more than two teams involved. Since Battlefests are "every team for itself" affairs, you can have as many as five enemy ships in the fray at any time. You need to prioritize your targets to deal out effective damage and extend your survival as long as possible.

Try to isolate a single target and concentrate your fire on that ship. This is especially important early on when you have minimal firepower. You cannot inflict any significant damage if you keep changing targets—plus, you incur the wrath of multiple enemies, making *your* ship the brunt of the attack. The best way to prevent this from happening is to give your enemies plenty to shoot at. Dive right into the fray and make sure there are plenty of potential targets around you at any given time (see Figure 14.3). Failing that, launch your shuttles to give your opponents something else to shoot at. This tactic works for human and AI players alike. Most players prefer to take out shuttle-craft shortly after they're launched to prevent unexpected damage from these nearly invisible attackers as the battle wears on.

> **TIP**
>
> *The more players you include in a skirmish, the bigger the map needs to be. Six-player games on small maps leave very little room to maneuver.*

The more teams there are, the more difficult things become. Your targeting priorities are as follows:

1. Ships that present the most imminent threat.

2. Ships that are easy marks (weaklings).

3. Ships that other teams/players are ganging up on.

> **TIP**
>
> *A Battlefest is one mission type in which self-destructing is a valid option. If you're near death and aren't on your last ship, you can use your ship's explosion to significantly weaken enemies, leaving your opponents much more vulnerable when you move in with your next ship.*

If it's at all possible, you're better off critically wounding ships than killing them. If you can damage enemies sufficiently to keep them off your tail, you have fewer enemies to worry about. If you kill your opponents, you have *bigger* enemies to worry about!

In a multi-team Battlefest, success often comes down to luck. If the other teams decide to pick on you (a *very* common situation in multiplayer Battlefests), all the starship command skill in the world won't save you.

Above all, remember that in a Battlefest, there are no points for style, and it doesn't matter how many ships you personally destroy. All that matters is that you be the last one standing.

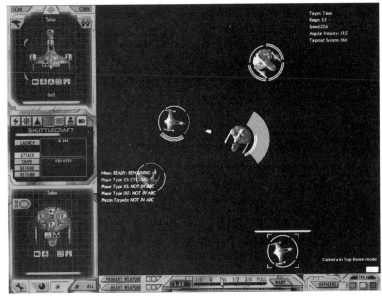

Figure 14.3 Keep your friends close and your enemies closer. Stay in the crowd so your enemies have plenty of targets besides you.

FREE FOR ALL

Rules and Objectives

Teams:	Up to 6
Ship Selection/Customization Allowed?	Yes
Mission Description:	An all-out brawl ensues until one team is left standing. Each player spawns at a random position as designated by the green icons on the map (which is displayed on the Setup screen).
End Conditions:	Last team/player standing wins.

Like Battlefests, Free for Alls can be played in teams or as individuals. When it's one-on-one, this type of mission is simply a ship-to-ship duel to the death. Configured in this manner, the Free for All is a great way to practice your tactics against various enemies, and to test new designs and new weapon types. Use the tips and tricks in Chapter 3 to get you through the battle and you should do well.

In a team game in which you have one or more wingman, divide and conquer. Separating and going after different opponents prevents them from ganging up on one of your ships and taking it out early.

When there are six players in an "every ship for itself" battle royal, your strategy in this skirmish type must be different than the one you use in a Battlefest because you don't have any ships to fall back on if you fail—when you're dead, you're out of the game.

TIP

To make things interesting, set a reasonable point limit for ships in a Free for All; 20,000–30,000 is a good range. Anybody can max out a ship, but it takes real skill to build an economical and effective combat starship.

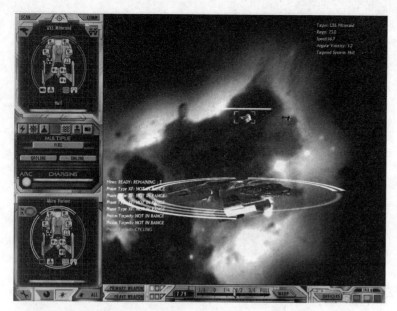

Caution is the keyword when you have no allies. Hang back when possible and let your opponents duke it out for a while (see Figure 14.4). Take evasive action when attacked and stay out of the fray until everyone has taken at least some damage. Then, move in and take advantage of your enemies' weakest shields, staying out of their strongest firing arcs when possible. As in a Battlefest, concentrate on one target at a time rather than minimizing your striking potential by spreading your damage over multiple ships. Once again, shuttlecraft are your friends: Stock up before the mission so you have plenty of additional targets to draw fire away from your ship.

Figure 14.4 When you have no allies, stay out of the battle as long as you can and take advantage of the damage inflicted on others by your opponents.

TEAM ASSAULT

Rules and Objectives

Teams:	2
Ship Selection/Customization Allowed?	Yes
Mission Description:	Both teams try to destroy each other's starbase. Ships respawn on destruction or disengagement.
End Conditions:	The player with a starbase remaining is the winner.

Team Assault is one of the most interesting skirmish missions available. The mission is unique in that you're both attacking an enemy starbase *and* defending a friendly starbase simultaneously. This calls for ships that can take a pounding and dish out huge amounts of damage in each salvo. Choose the best ships that the points allow for this mission and equip them with heavy shields and high-power weapons on the Refit screen.

This mission is a real challenge when it comes to sorting your priorities. Against the AI, protecting your base usually isn't a problem. The enemy defenders place a higher priority on defending their own base than on attacking yours. That means you can keep your base safe simply by doing your duty and assaulting the enemy installation. This tends to work in any situation against the AI where there is a one-to-one ratio of defenders to attackers.

In a multiplayer game, you can't count on your enemy being so accommodating. One-on-one multiplayer Team Assaults are usually a race to see whose ship can wipe out the enemy base first. If there are multiple players on each team, leave at least one ship behind to guard the base while the rest of the team spearheads the assault.

The map you choose determines the mood of the skirmish. In open space, especially on a small map, a Team Assault invariably turns into an all-out battle with few subtle tactics involved. To add to the interest and strategy of the scenario, choose a large map, preferably one with asteroids. On a large map, you can't target the enemy base or defenders at the start of the mission; you have to go looking for them. Hunting for enemy ships is a lot more challenging if there are asteroids to hide behind (see Figure 14.5). On large maps, you can also use the enemy's sensor-range limitations to your advantage. Skirt the edge of the map on your way across to hide from enemy sensors rather than approaching the enemy base in a headlong rush and revealing your intentions immediately.

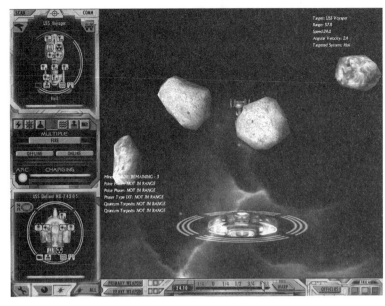

Figure 14.5 If there are asteroids in the area, keep them between you and the enemy to mask your approach.

Perhaps the most interesting feature of the Team Assault skirmish is that when a ship is destroyed or disengages from the map, it respawns moments later—*fully repaired and intact*—and can rejoin the fight. This presents some unique opportunities that are unavailable in any other mission type:

WARNING

When you decide to disengage or self-destruct to get a fresh ship, be certain that's really what you want to do. Your ship respawns in one of the map corners on your base's side of the sector (see Figure 14.6). You have to traverse a considerable distance—especially on a big map—to rejoin the battle.

Ship "trade-ins": If your ship is beaten up beyond all hope of survival, you can disengage and get a shiny new one.

Suicide runs: Team Assault is another mission type in which self-destructing is a valuable tactic. If your ship is badly damaged, set the self-destruct and move in close to the enemy base. When your warp core blows, it should do some serious damage to the base's shields (or to the base itself if the shields are down).

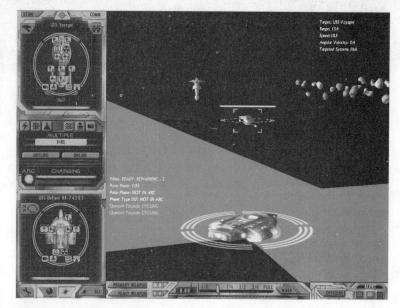

The usual base assault tactic of dealing with the defending ships first and then fighting the base is considerably less effective in a Team Assault because of the ship-respawning feature. On large maps, taking out the defending ships does give you a bit of breathing room (especially if you destroy them on *your* side of the map), but on smaller maps, the enemy ships are back in the fray seconds after they're destroyed.

Figure 14.6 In a Team Assault, you have eternal life—but it takes you a while to get back in the fight after you respawn.

15

Dynaverse 3

In addition to the single-player campaign discussed earlier in this guide, *Starfleet Command III* includes Dynaverse 3—a multiplayer online campaign in which hundreds of starship commanders can take to the stars for the glory of their respective empires.

In many ways, a Dynaverse game plays like a Conquest campaign. Your goal is to take over as much of the galaxy as possible, however, the dynamics of the game are quite different in Dynaverse because it introduces the most unpredictable element of all: the human factor. Although you still fight some battles against AI opponents, many of the skirmishes you engage in are against other Dynaverse players.

This chapter provides an overview of Dynaverse 3 and offers suggestions and strategies to improve your online campaign experience.

WHAT TO EXPECT IN THE DYNAVERSE

"Destroying an empire to win a war is no victory, and losing a battle to save an empire is no defeat."—Kahless

When you engage other humans in combat for the first time, you're likely to find that fighting the AI was a cakewalk by comparison. Some things that you should expect from human opponents include the following:

Customized ships: You don't often encounter many surprises when it comes to ship configuration in a single-player campaign. In the Dynaverse, however, you must expect the unexpected. Your opponents are just as likely to upgrade their weapons as you are, so note the enemy ship configuration before you form your battle strategy. Also, expect your enemies to make heavier use of nontraditional heavy weapons. Tachyon pulses, ion cannons, and antimatter mines are a lot more common online.

Unpredictable tactics: After you've gained some experience in single-player, you'll probably find that the AI's maneuvers (and reactions to your maneuvers) become somewhat predictable. When you're up against humans, expect your enemies to adapt to your tactics more readily and to use a myriad of unpredictable tactics of their own.

Fleets: One of the nicest features of Dynaverse 3 is the ability to easily form a fleet with other players on your team. Expect to encounter enemies in groups rather than singly. A group of unpredictable humans fighting as a team is a lot more dangerous than a ragtag collection of AI ships.

GOALS AND VICTORY CONDITIONS

Dynaverse campaigns are, simultaneously, cooperative and competitive ventures. You're working *with* other players in your empire and *against* players in other empires. Your ultimate goal is to capture and hold the most map sectors (hexes). You do this by battling in enemy or neutral territory.

TIP

When an empire is close to achieving an economic victory, all players receive a message notifying them of this fact. When you receive such a message (and your empire isn't the one in the lead), it's time to start aggressively attacking the leading empire and taking away their sectors to reduce their economic advantage.

The sheer number of hexes your empire controls isn't the only way your empire can win. The Dynaverse also uses an economic system to determine victors. Every sector has an economic value, which is displayed when you scan (right-click on) the hex. At the end of each time cycle (when the game clock below the map/news area changes to the next "date"), the game checks the relative economic value of the territory held by all empires. If your empire's economic point total is higher than all the other empires' *combined* total, your empire wins.

Losing is a lot more straightforward in most cases. If, at any point in the game, your empire has lost control of all its sectors, your empire is eliminated from the game.

DYNAVERSE MISSIONS

Dynaverse missions are discovered in much the same way as Conquest campaign missions. Scan the surrounding sectors for enemy activity—ships, bases, planets, and so on—and engage the enemy at will. Your goal is to capture enemy territory, so it behooves you to seek out battles in neutral or enemy territory. If you see enemy ships in *your* empire's territory, however, make them a top priority. Remember that all the other empires have the same goals of conquest as you.

You're often presented with number of different attack options when you go to the mission screen. You start the game with a frigate—the weakest ship available—so make sure to select a

mission your ship can handle. Even when you have moved on to a better vessel, keep your limitations in mind. Losing a ship in a Dynaverse game is devastating, especially after you've upgraded the ship and weapons. It takes a while to build up enough prestige to buy a good ship, and you start over with a weak frigate every time your ship is destroyed.

When it comes to defending your empire, the news feed is a vital tool (see Figure 15.1). Here, you can check on enemy activity all over the galaxy and determine where your opponents are making moves against your sectors. If you see a massive push in a given area, rally some support and head over to the beleaguered sectors to mount a defense.

When choosing sectors to attack, keep the economic factor of the game in mind, and choose your target sector based on its economic value. Remember that your empire can win by having the strongest economy or the most sectors under its control.

As in the single-player campaigns, you're awarded prestige for completing Dynaverse missions. The amount of prestige you're awarded depends on the difficulty of the mission—the number of enemy ships and installations present, the relative strength of the enemy ships compared with yours, and so on. The rule of

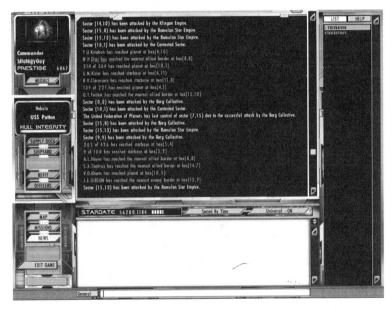

Figure 15.1 Check the news regularly to monitor enemy offensive action.

> NOTE
>
> *When a friendly ship or installation comes under attack, you have a finite amount of time to respond and lend a hand in the attack. If you miss that window of opportunity to join in the battle, your allies must fend for themselves.*

181

Dynaverse Missions

NOTE

Most of the missions in Dynaverse games are very similar to the general campaign missions in single-player campaigns. Check out the strategies in Chapter 14 for tips and strategies.

thumb is that harder missions provide more prestige. As is true in the general campaign missions in the single-player campaign, you're much better off retreating from a battle than if you stick it out and lose. You lose prestige only when your ship is destroyed.

When you disengage from battle before the mission is completed, both your ship and that of the enemy remain in their post-battle condition until repaired and re-supplied at a base. Try to keep track of enemy targets after you disengage. If you can call in reinforcements before the enemy reaches a base, your team can re-engage the enemy ship while it's still in its weakened state.

FLEETS

One of the most important cooperative aspects of Dynaverse campaigns is the formation of fleets. When you enter a sector that contains other friendly vessels, you can join with those vessels (or they can join with you) and form a fleet. Fleets travel together on the map (the fleet leader controls the movement), and engage in battle together when they attack or are attacked.

Fleets provide a tremendous advantage, especially early in the game when your ship is small and weak (see Figure 15.2). Fleets are also vital when engaging in large-scale assaults against enemy starbases, planets, and fleets.

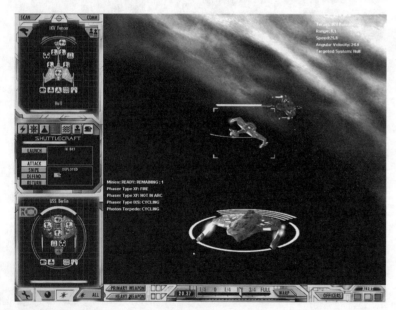

When you're asked to join a fleet, you should always consider it, and if you see that no one in your empire is taking advantage of fleet actions, you should offer to form a fleet with them. The advantages of working together as a team far outweigh the constricted freedom of moving with a group. Besides, you can always leave the fleet whenever you want, or disband it if you're the lead ship.

Figure 15.2 Fighting as a fleet improves your chances of survival early in the game.

REFITS AND SHIP UPGRADES

In the targ-eat-targ world of the Dynaverse campaign, ship refits and upgrades take on even greater importance than in a single-player campaign. You start with a default-configuration frigate—and you really can't do a lot with a ship that small. Your first goal, before you even enter your first battle, is to upgrade your weapons and systems to make your frigate a little more likely to survive.

Use your initial prestige to max out your weapons, shields, and armor so that you can take on some easy missions and start accumulating additional prestige. Keep an eye on the ship prices whenever you're in a sector with a base, and as soon as you have enough prestige, ditch that frigate and get yourself a bigger ship.

NOTE

After you refit or upgrade your ship, you get to keep that ship even if you log off and rejoin the same game at a later time. All your accumulated prestige also follows you from session to session (but not from one Dynaverse game to another).

Surviving the Ship Auction

Although refitting ships is no different in a Dynaverse campaign than it is in the single-player version, purchasing new ships is handled in a completely different manner.

When you visit the shipyard, you can browse the ships just as you would in the single-player campaign, but instead of a simple ship and price list, you're presented with a list of ships and the opening or current *bids* for each. In Dynaverse games, there are a finite number of ships available at any given time, and you must bid against other players on your team to purchase them.

A ship auction begins when you or another player place a bid on one of the available ships. You can up your bid by a fixed number of prestige points or by a percentage of the current price. Each auction lasts for several game cycles (the ending date of the auction is displayed on the shipyard screen). When you're involved in an auction, keep checking back to see if you've been outbid. When the auction ends, the winner's current ship is immediately replaced with the new ship, unless the winning bidder is engaged in battle, in which case, their ship is replaced after the battle ends.

Check out Chapters 4–7 and familiarize yourself with the actual value of each ship type so that you know about how much each hull class is actually worth. The rule of thumb in any auction is to set an upper limit on what you're willing to pay and stick to it. There's no need to pay more than the ship is worth. Other ships will eventually be available, so don't waste your prestige.

You can actually use some other real-world auction tactics to secure the ship that you want. For example, note the end time of the auction and don't place a bid until the auction is moments from ending. That way, you get the high bid in and the other bidders have no time to place a counter-bid. Use this tactic sparingly, though. You're supposed to be working together, after all, and "sniping" an ally's ship auction is no way to engender good will among teammates.

A friendlier tactic is to pick a time when few of your teammates are logged in to bid on a ship. If there's no competition, the ship is yours without a fight.

Buying Bases

Although you can buy bases in single-player campaigns, there is little need to do so (at least, not in the story-based campaigns). In Dynaverse games, purchasing bases and defense platforms is a vital part of your team's strategy.

WARNING

When you buy a base, remember that you must place the base in a friendly sector before it becomes functional. Avoid confrontations before you deploy the base. If your ship is destroyed before the base is placed, the base is lost, along with all the prestige you spent on it.

First, the presence of a base makes it more difficult for an enemy to take control of a sector. For this reason, placing numerous bases in border areas is an excellent way to slow enemy expansion into your territory. Bases near enemy borders also provide repair, refit, and re-supply points for allied vessels. By providing facilities near the border, you eliminate the need for allied fleets to limp across your entire empire to repair their damage, an activity that wastes time and leaves ships vulnerable for extended periods of time.

Because they cost you a lot of prestige, buying a base is a major humanitarian gesture on your part. You're encouraged to make such a gesture. Remember, everything you do for the betterment of the team benefits you as well. Before you start spending prestige frivolously, however, you must see to your own needs. Until you have upgraded your ship to at least a battlecruiser-class vessel, don't consider buying bases. A strong, mobile fleet is ultimately more important to your empire's cause than bases.

Use the chat feature of the game to discuss base purchase and placement with your teammates. By coordinating your base purchase and placement efforts, you can optimize base deployment and save each other lots of prestige.

TIP

Bases are bought at auction just as starships are. You should never get into a bidding war for a base, though. Because the base benefits your entire team, there is no logic whatsoever in trying to outbid another team member for a base.

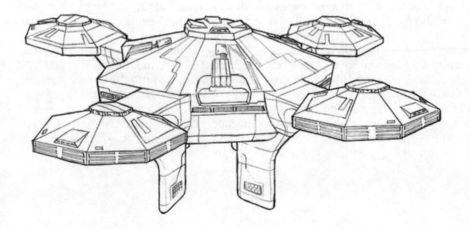

Appendix

Non-Player Craft and Installations

The following tables contain the statistics for all non-player craft and installations you might encounter in the game—shuttlecraft, freighters, alien starships, starbases, and so on. Note that some of these stats might be altered in certain scenarios—only the default configurations for each vessel and installation are provided here.

Weapon Abbreviations

Phaser: P

Klingon Disruptor: D

Romulan Disruptor: RD

Cutting Beam: C
(LC = light cutting beam, and so on)

Photon Torpedo: PT

Klingon Photon Torpedo: KPT

Quantum Torpedo: QT

Plasma Torpedo: PLT
(L-PLT = light plasma torpedo, and so on)

Gravimetric Torpedo: GT

Polaron Torpedo: POT

Myotronic Beam: MB

Tachyon Pulse: TP

Shield Inversion Beam: SB

Ion Cannon: IC

Nuclear Mine: MN

Ship	Shield Type	Armor Type	Cloak	Primary Weapons	Heavy Weapons
Federation Shuttlecraft	None	None	None	P-IXS (1)	None
Federation Freighter	I	I	None	P-XS (1)	None
Klingon Shuttlecraft	None	None	None	D-I (1)	None
Klingon Freighter	I	I	None	D-II (1)	None
Romulan Shuttlecraft	None	None	None	RD-I (1)	None
Romulan Freighter	I	I	None	RD-II (1)	None
Borg Shuttlecraft	None	None	None	LC (1)	None
Borg Freighter (Cylinder)	I	I	None	LC (1)	None

Table A.1 Shuttlecraft and Freighters

Ship	Shield Type	Armor Type	Cloak	Primary Weapons	Heavy Weapons
Marauder	I	None	None	D-IF (2)	PT (2)

Table A.2 Ferengi Ships

Ship	Shield Type	Armor Type	Cloak	Primary Weapons	Heavy Weapons
Attack Ship	I	I	None	P-XS (1)	None
Light Cruiser	I	I	None	P-XS (2)	None

Table A.3 Rakellian Ships

Ship	Shield Type	Armor Type	Cloak	Primary Weapons	Heavy Weapons
Frigate	I	I	None	P-XS (2)	None
Cruiser	I	I	None	P-XS (2)	PT (2)

Table A.4 Pirate ships

Ship	Shield Type	Armor Type	Cloak	Primary Weapons	Heavy Weapons
Galor-Class	III	III	None	P-XS (2)	KPT (2)
Keldon-Class	V	III	Yes	P-XIS (2)	KPT (3)

Table A.5 Cardassian ships

Installation	Shield Type	Armor Type	Cloak	Primary Weapons	Heavy Weapons
Stardock	None	I	None	None	None
Listening Post	None	I	None	None	None
Defense Platform	I	I	None	P-XS (1)	PT (1)
Asteroid Base	I	I	None	P-XS (1)	PT (1)
Basestation	V	V	None	P-XIIIS (3)	QT (3)
Battlestation	V	V	None	P-XIIIS (4)	QT (4)
Starbase	V	V	None	P-XIIIS (6)	QT (6)

Table A.6 Federation installations

Installation	Shield Type	Armor Type	Cloak	Primary Weapons	Heavy Weapons
Stardock	None	I	None	None	None
Listening Post	None	I	None	None	None
Defense Platform	I	I	None	D-III (1)	KPT (1)
Asteroid Base	I	I	None	D-V (1)	KPT (1)
Basestation	V	V	None	D-V (3)	KPT (3)
Battlestation	V	V	None	D-V (4)	KPT (4)
Starbase	V	V	None	D-V (6)	KPT (6)

Table A.7 Klingon Installations

Installation	Shield Type	Armor Type	Cloak	Primary Weapons	Heavy Weapons
Stardock	None	I	None	None	None
Listening Post	None	I	None	None	None
Defense Platform	I	I	None	RD-III (1)	M-PLT (1)
Asteroid Base	I	I	None	RD-III (1)	M-PLT (1)
Basestation	V	V	None	RD-V (3)	H-PLT (3)
Battlestation	V	V	None	RD-V (4)	H-PLT (4)
Starbase	V	V	None	RD-V (6)	H-PLT (6)

Table A.8 Romulan installations

Appendix: Non-Player Craft and Installations

Installation	Shield Type	Armor Type	Cloak	Primary Weapons	Heavy Weapons
Stardock	N/A	I	None	None	None
Listening Post	N/A	I	None	None	None
Defense Platform	N/A	I	None	MC (1)	GT (1)
Asteroid Base	N/A	I	None	HC (1)	GT (1)
Basestation	N/A	V	None	HC (3)	GT (3)
Battlestation	N/A	V	None	HC (4)	GT (4)
Starbase	N/A	V	None	HC (6)	GT (6)

Table A.9 Borg installations

Installation	Shield Type	Armor Type	Cloak	Primary Weapons	Heavy Weapons
Rakellian Listening Post	None	I	None	None	None
Rakellian Defense Platform	I	I	None	D-III (1)	None
Rakellian Asteroid Base	I	I	None	D-V (1)	PT (1)

Table A.10 Rakellian installations

Appendix: Non-Player Craft and Installations